Angela,

Wishing you
mentoring success!

Best Wishes,

Hayley

10 - 18 - 17

THE
CAREER
COMPASS

**Mentoring to Point You Toward Maximum
Professional and Personal Growth**

SECOND EDITION

HAYLEY NORMAN
STEPHANIE MELNICK

Marin-Valdes Publishing
Tampa, FL

Published by
Marin-Valdes Publishing
Tampa, FL

Publisher's Cataloging-in-Publication Data
Norman, Hayley A. and Melnick, Stephanie M.

ISBN: 978-0-9977695-0-0 (Hardcover)
ISBN: 978-0-9977695-1-7 (Paperback)

Second Edition

This book is dedicated to all of the mentors who have inspired us along our individual and collective career journeys. Without their guidance, support, and continued encouragement this book would not have been possible.

TABLE OF CONTENTS

ACKNOWLEDGMENTS

The song "For Good" from the Broadway show *Wicked* summarizes how impactful a mentoring relationship can be.

"I've heard it said
That people come into our lives for a reason
Bringing something we must learn
And we are led
To those who help us most to grow
If we let them
And we help them in return
Well, I don't know if I believe that's true
But I know I'm who I am today
Because I knew you…"

We are blessed to have been mentored by many talented and generous individuals. These friends, family members and leaders have positively impacted our lives and our professional development, and have pushed us to accomplish great things.

Hayley's Mentors

Mr. Robinson, my high school music teacher, taught me that I could accomplish anything with hard work and passion. He inspired me to stretch myself beyond my preconceived boundaries and gave me the confidence to connect with an audience.

My professors at the University of Tampa, Helene Silverman and Ed Clourtier, fueled my desire for helping others reach their full potential. Dr. Silverman knew that I could do more and pushed me to higher levels by providing opportunities outside of the classroom for me to grow. Dr. Clourtier was always available to offer insights, encouragement and advice. Although it has been over 27 years since I walked across the stage with my diploma, I still meet Ed from time to time for a good cup of coffee and advice. Dr. Clourtier is a forever mentor!

Many strong women in my life have inspired me along my career journey. Sandy Rice inspired me to bring the process of mentoring to many. Dawn Brehm supported and guided me through the sometimes rough waters of corporate America. I am so fortunate to have had these two strong women in my life as mentors and life-long friends.

Finally, to the person who once said, when I doubted my abilities, "Everything that you have is everything we need," and helped me realize and claim my God given strengths…Stephanie, I am eternally grateful for the opportunity to partner with you on this unbelievable adventure. I am constantly astonished by your talents. You amaze, encourage and mentor me every single day!

Stephanie's Mentors

Mrs. Jordan, my high school journalism teacher, may not remember the name Stephanie Torrens, but I remember her. She noticed my love for writing and encouraged me to use my talents and take big risks.

Mr. James Haskins, the toughest of all my professors at the University of Florida, challenged me to be a better thinker and writer, and encouraged me to be brave and stand up for what I believed in. He was a prolific and courageous author who wrote the book *The Cotton Club*, among many others. At first, I was terrified of him. He welcomed us to Adolescent Literature by stating that only one-fifth of us might survive his class. He was formidable, and I was privileged to know him. He passed away in 2005.

Kent Rattey was perhaps my most reluctant mentor. He challenged me to join him at the bar for happy hour each day until I had mastered his lessons on the art of business and credit while working for Dun & Bradstreet. It was my greatest learning ground and one of the best times of my life.

Rick Beller has, without a doubt, been one of my most influential mentors and kindest friends. He has guided me in business every step of the way, never asking for anything in return. When I initially shared the idea of building my own consulting firm, he encouraged me. He helped me land my first clients, and continues to be a trusted mentor and friend today.

Although I have had many mentors in my life, Hayley Norman has been the greatest among them. She has moved me out of my comfort zone, pushed me to expose my hidden talents, and helped me overcome some of my greatest fears. There are not enough words to thank her.

We Are Grateful

We came together to form Metajourn on March 1, 2012. Since then we have faced many daunting challenges and have been blessed with exciting opportunities. Pastors Tony and Kaci Stewart have mentored us spiritually, reminding us to use our gifts, celebrate life, give back to others and stand with undying conviction. Nancy Latham is a favorite client and fabulous friend who embodies vision, persistence, and above all things faith. She models those unique and fabulous attributes with the highest degree of grace, and we are privileged to know her. And Mike Petrilli – a man with a tough exterior, but an incredibly kind heart – who reminds us that smooth seas do not make skillful sailors. It is always fun being part of the crew. Finally, a special and humble man who has supported us in so many ways that it is difficult to summarize them in a few simple sentences. Suffice to say he is truly an amazing man and, to him, we are eternally grateful. He knows who he is.

We'd like to thank our parents, perhaps our first and most loyal mentors, who taught us about the power of belief and the importance of hard work. They are loving, yet appropriately critical. Ultimately, we are who we are because of them. We'd also like to thank our spouses, David and Matt, for supporting our crazy ideas without hesitation, and for managing our lives and families while we worked late hours at the office. Finally, we'd like to thank our beautiful and talented children – Davin, Kimi, Abby and Jack – for loving us unconditionally and always keeping us humble.

PROLOGUE

We published the first edition of *The Career Compass: Mentoring to Point You Toward Maximum Professional and Personal Growth* in 2011. At that time, formal mentoring in a corporate environment was still in its infancy. Companies were investing in sophisticated systems to match mentors with mentees, and there was a lot of buzz on the topic. However, despite the best efforts of these companies, employee expectations often exceeded realized results.

Both mentors and mentees pointed to the lack of available education, lack of structure, and lack of discipline as some of the factors that contributed to their dissatisfaction. Thankfully, much has changed in a few short years, as the world has become more aware of the benefits of mentoring. We are happy to say that now, five years after publishing our first edition of The Career Compass, mentoring has found its place among the talent strategies of top companies and institutions around the world.

We wrote *The Career Compass* to provide guidance and direction for both the mentor and the mentee, and to help build a common language between them. Our mentoring model provides a disciplined approach to building a mentoring relationship, and serves as a diagnostic for mentors and mentees who may find themselves stuck as they work toward their goals. The questions and assessments help both parties prepare to benefit from their time together, and the tips and traps help mentors and mentees stay out of harm's way.

We wrote the second edition of *The Career Compass* to acknowledge the evolution of mentoring, and to share new insights, observations and best practices from our own experiences and from the experiences of our clients around the world.

Mentoring has changed...

- Mentoring is growing within the corporate setting *and* expanding beyond business. In addition to corporate institutions, we now implement formalized mentoring in higher education, public and private school systems, religious and community organizations, and professional associations.

- Organizations of all sizes – for profit and not-for-profit, public and private – are implementing informal and formal mentoring programs. Today, three out of four Fortune 500 companies have formal mentoring programs.

- Organizations are using mentoring strategically to grow and develop their best talent. Mentoring continues to be a key driver of diversity and inclusion efforts. In fact, Diversity Inc. recognizes the value of cutting-edge diversity-management techniques, and recently raised the importance of mentoring participation in the selection of The Diversity Inc. Top 50.

- New positions and job roles have emerged to support the increasing number, and expanded scope, of mentoring programs. We now work with Mentoring Managers, Mentoring Program Coordinators, Executive Directors of Mentoring, and Directors of Diversity and Inclusion, among others

- There is now clear differentiation between the roles of coaches, mentors, and sponsors. The distinctions have led to a better understanding of what mentoring is and isn't, and have fostered higher levels of employee satisfaction among program participants.

In response to the changes, we have further refined our definitions of coaching, mentoring and sponsorship to help further clarify the roles, and to codify the respective benefits of each relationship type. We have also enhanced our mentoring model to make it easier to understand, share and use. Finally, we've added some new stories about mentors and mentees in hopes they will inspire you as you embark on your own mentoring journey.

Mentoring Definitions

There was a time when mentoring was characterized as a "sustained relationship between a younger, less experienced individual (protégé) and an older, more experienced individual (mentor) dedicated to achieving long term success and fulfillment." However, that definition is now dated.

Experts suggest that the essence of mentoring involves tapping into the knowledge of others to improve one's life, and most acknowledge that successful mentoring relationships stand to benefit both the mentor and the mentee. While a mentee may gain valuable career advice and guidance, their mentor may learn about the needs of a new generation and may obtain insights about how to transform the company for the future. Mentoring is a gift that both the mentor and the mentee can share long after their initial meetings.

Mentors can be young or old, men or women, and come from any level in an organization, institution or community. In your lifetime, you may have one or many. According to the Oxford Dictionaries, a mentor is "an experienced trusted advisor." A corporate executive with 30 years in the business may turn to a Millennial to be mentored in the disciplines and practices of social media. While a young new hire might seek career advice from a veteran leader who has "been there and done that."

About the Book

The Career Compass was written for readers in search of a mentor *and* for those looking to give back to mentees. The front half of the book is dedicated to the mentor, and the second half to the mentee. Regardless of your intention, you may benefit from reading the book in its entirety.

The book is a how-to,what's-next read, filled with questions, activities and exercises. You may choose to write directly on its pages, or capture your thoughts in a companion journal of your choosing. Whatever you decide, we hope *The Career Compass* will be a trusted advisor and go-to resource for all things mentoring.

If you are lucky, you will have many mentors in your life, and it is our hope that you will take time to share your gifts by mentoring others. Whether you aspire to *be* a mentor or to have one, a mentoring relationship just might change your life.

Embrace the journey!
Hayley and Stephanie

INTRODUCTION

"Mentor: Someone whose hindsight can become your foresight."
–Anonymous

Most of us are mentored in one form or another, personally or professionally, at some point in our lives. At home, our parents mentor us, modeling morals and values. At school, our teachers mentor us, guiding us through new concepts and encouraging appropriate study habits. Religious leaders mentor us, neighbors mentor us.

Henry David Thoreau had Ralph Waldo Emerson. Helen Keller had Anne Sullivan. Oprah Winfrey had Mrs. Duncan, her fourth grade teacher. Dr. Martin Luther King had Dr. Benjamin Mays, and Luke Skywalker had Obi-Wan Kenobi. Many well-known politicians, entrepreneurs, business professionals, entertainers, community activists, inventors and artists were shaped by mentors somewhere along the way.

Mentors offer guidance and observation without control. They provide professional and emotional support based on their own experiences. The relationship between a mentor and a mentee is special because everyone benefits: the mentor, the mentee, and the institutions and organizations with which the individuals are involved.

Coaching, Mentoring and Sponsorship

Since writing the first edition of *The Career Compass*, the definitions of coaching, mentoring, and sponsorship have become more clearly delineated. You may be a coach, a mentor, or a sponsor. Or, you may need a coach, a mentor, or a sponsor. In fact, you may be, or need, all three at some point in your career or life. We've found that understanding the distinction between these three unique roles can help you find the perfect person to help you on your journey, or to find a mentee who could benefit from your experience. In short, a coach builds skill, a mentor shares advice and experience, and a sponsor advocates on your behalf.

As we were putting the final touches on this second edition of *The Career Compass*, we were also beginning a new project focused on Sponsorship. In our latest book, *CLIMB, Harnessing the Power of Sponsorship to Reach Your Career Summit,* we use a metaphor to describe the differences between a coach, a mentor and a sponsor. You might be catching on to the fact that we love a good metaphor and are slightly obsessed with those related to travel. We also have an affinity for Mount Everest and the people of Tibet. So, a visual metaphor related to mountain climbing seemed fitting. (Figure 1)

Figure 1

People often talk about reaching the summit or pinnacle of a career. When you think about resources who can help you conquer your goals, imagine traversing your career as if you were climbing a mountain...

As you head to the mountain to begin your climb, you'll need a Global Positioning System (GPS) to give you turn-by-turn directions. Without a GPS, you could start out in the wrong direction or take the wrong route, which could make reaching your destination difficult. You might make a wrong turn and unknowingly head into dangerous territory. Think of a coach in the business world as your GPS. A coach is someone who gives you a specific set of instructions to help you master a task, and helps you by providing frequent step-by-step guidance. You might need a coach as you take on a new position or are asked to work on a special project that requires you to learn a new set of skills.

When you find yourself at the base of the mountain, ready to begin the trek to the top, you'll no longer require turn-by-turn directions from a GPS. Instead, you'll likely need a compass that can ensure that you are directionally correct. A mentor is like a compass – a career compass – that helps to guide you along a path, and helps to redirect you, if you happen to veer too far to the East or West. A good mentor will have travelled the path you intend to travel, and will be able to advise you as you complete your own climb. Mentors offer guidance for growth and development.

Once you've reached the highest base camp, there's just one thing left to do…ascend to the summit. Any experienced climber knows that the key to making it to the top is to have a wise Sherpa by their side. In real life, Sherpas are highly respected, elite mountaineers who serve as guides on treacherous climbing expeditions. They risk their own lives to make sure that climbers make it safely to the top. A sponsor is like a Sherpa in the corporate world. The sponsor's job is to help you reach your summit, in this case, your personal or career goal. Although over 4,000 people have scaled the summit of Mount Everest, only one, Reinhold Messner, did it without the assistance of a Sherpa. Similarly, corporate mountain climbers rarely make it to the top without some help. So, never be too proud or too embarrassed to ask for it.

Mentoring is not like coaching or sponsorship. A mentor's primary role is not to provide step-by-step directions, or to advocate on another's behalf. Instead, it's the mentor's job to provide guidance to help the mentee reach their full potential.

Value for Mentors

While it may appear that mentees have the most to gain through mentoring, there are plenty of great rewards for mentors. Mentors can benefit from:

- Enhancing their people development skills

- Sharing the breadth of their experience

- Transferring corporate culture to the next generation

- Developing next-level leaders

- Leaving a legacy

- Learning from the mentee

- Gaining inner satisfaction

- Learning from others

- Gaining renewed energy and inspiration

Value for Mentees

For mentees, the advantages of having a mentor include:

- The opportunity to explore different career options

- Accelerated career development

- Honest feedback to help break through boundaries and fears

- Improved interpersonal skills

- Increased knowledge in areas outside one's expertise

- Expanded networking opportunities

- Enhanced job satisfaction

- A safe place to share politically sensitive issues and receive sound advice

- Improved problem-solving skills

Value for the Organization

Throughout the book, you'll see references to the organization, institution or company, but mentoring is not confined to a specific construct. Mentoring can thrive in almost any environment: in education, in the community, within a church or synagogue, etc. Mentoring can occur anywhere, and interactions are not limited to face-to-face meetings. Today's mentors and mentees are creative. They find ways to work across borders, time zones and technologies.

Organizations with formal mentoring programs benefit from:

- High levels of employee engagement

- Accelerated development of key talent

- Retention of key talent

- Alignment to strategic imperatives

- Increased productivity

- A seamless and effective way to transfer corporate culture

Success Factors for Mentoring

There are many factors that contribute to a successful mentoring relationship. From our perspective, the most important are:

1. Chemistry and Trust

2. The "Right" Structure

3. Shared Expectations

4. A Skilled Mentor

Chemistry and trust. Chemistry and trust are critically important, as mentoring often centers around confidential conversations.

Chemistry makes it easy to share one's deepest thoughts and fears, and vet crazy ideas. Trust involves the confidence that an individual is good and honest, and that the environment for conversation is safe and secure.

Whether the mentoring relationship lasts an hour, a year, or a decade, chemistry and trust must be at its core. Both the mentor and mentee must feel comfortable being transparent and forthright with each other. When chemistry and trust are lacking, information may be withheld by either party as a means of self-protection. For example, a mentee may hesitate to disclose a critical mistake or error in judgment that the mentor could help to resolve. Likewise, the mentor may hesitate to admit that they made a similar mistake. Time can be wasted and faulty advice given, when chemistry and trust are lacking.

That said...don't be too worried if chemistry and trust don't exist at the outset of a relationship. Whether you're hoping to become a mentor or a mentee, know that chemistry and trust can be developed over time. We've seen some pretty rocky partnerships develop into relationships of true respect and admiration.

The "right" structure. The old adage, "Form follows function," is certainly relevant when it comes to mentoring. The form and structure of the mentorship should align with the goals for the mentoring relationship. Therefore, it is important for both the mentor and mentee to be clear about their objectives and intentions. Although there are many mentoring structures, mentor/mentee pairings represent the most common type of mentoring relationships. Many organizations have formal mentoring programs that match mentors with mentees based on skills, interests, and/or goals. Some organizations offer less formal programs that simply encourage mentee/mentor pairings. When no program exists, it is up to the individuals to develop and cultivate relationships on their own.

But mentoring structures are not limited strictly to partnerships. For example, a single individual may mentor a group of mentees with common goals, or a collective of mentors may work with a group of like-minded individuals pursuing similar objectives. Group mentoring allows a mentor and several mentees to problem-solve and network for everyone's benefit.

Top-down mentoring is still quite common, but mentoring partnerships are not always based on hierarchical relationships. Peer-to-peer mentoring by like-level colleagues in the same organization is rising in popularity. Peers and peer groups benefit from information sharing, feedback, and the skills and perspectives of others with unique skills and experience. We are also seeing a trend toward "upside down" mentoring, when an individual whose title is lower on the organizational chart mentors someone with a higher position. This type of mentoring may involve the use of technologies that may be more familiar to someone actively involved in the discipline.

Shared expectations. Realistic goals and shared expectations go a long way toward creating relationships that are universally beneficial and rewarding. Relationships can fail if a mentee's expectations fail to align with their mentor's. For instance, a mentee hoping for a shortcut to a quick promotion could lose focus and abandon the process if their desired position is offered to someone else, and they have not set longer-term goals. For this reason, we recommend that the mentor and mentee work together to set expectations during the initial meeting. Taking the time upfront, creates a shared sense of ownership and establishes basic parameters for the relationship. We included a Mentoring Agreement in the resources section of this book to help get you started.

A skilled mentor. Many mentors come to the process with tons of experience under their belts. They may have had many mentees in the past, and may have learned how to effectively navigate a successful mentoring relationship. However, some mentors enter the process with the best of intentions, but little experience and no formal training. We have witnessed many a well-meaning mentor fall short of expectations due to a lack of knowledge and/or skill. But, we have also seen how mentor training can empower a mentor with the skills and abilities needed to form strong and lasting relationships.

An effective mentor training curriculum should focus on the unique aptitudes and attitudes needed to be a good mentor. (See chart on page 5–6.) While many of the aptitudes and attitudes may come naturally to some individuals, others may need to be developed. Identifying an individual's areas of strength and opportunities for development is a critical first step in preparing mentors for success.

In addition to developing the required aptitudes and attitudes, mentors and mentor candidates should also be exposed to the realities of mentoring before making a formal commitment to the process.

Challenging situations may occasionally arise between a mentor and their mentee. Realistic practice scenarios and simulations can help prepare mentors for the unexpected, and can help them anticipate and respond to some of the most common mentoring challenges. The right tools and resources give mentors access to support, if and when they need it.

A Journey, Not a Destination

When we wrote the first edition, we couldn't avoid thinking about mentoring as a journey: with peaks and valleys, forks in the road and potential detours, sunny days and gloomy days, rest stops and speed bumps. We reflected on our own mentoring experiences, and found that although some mentors were with us for only a fleeting moment, many guided us for long periods of time. Each journey, with each mentor, was different, in part, because each partnership was formed with a different intention. As we developed our mentoring model we thought about planning a trip for an amazing, yet potentially unpredictable, ride. (Figure 2)

The Mentoring Journey: A Practical Model

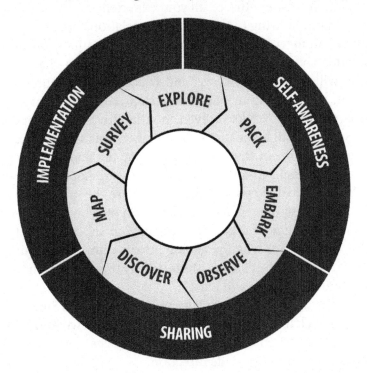

Figure 2

In an effort to compartmentalize the steps of the process, we added an outer ring to the original model. Each of the phases, Self-Awareness, Sharing, and Implementation, is critical to a successful mentorship. In combination, the phases help to ensure that both the mentor and the mentee are clear about the destination, have a reasonable and realistic plan to get there, and have a way to monitor their progress. If you follow the steps as you move through the phases of your own mentoring journey, you will increase the odds that you will arrive at your destination and enjoy the ride.

The chapters in this book are organized around the steps contained in the Mentoring Journey model, and are titled as such. Whether you are a mentor or mentee, or aspire to be one, the information and exercises will guide you through the process.

The first steps of the Mentoring Journey include **Explore** and **Pack**. These steps involve introspection, gathering information, and discussing aspirations. Your insights will provide the content for initial discussions with your mentor or mentee. During this phase, you will contemplate your strengths, recall your experiences, and consider what each of you might bring to the mentoring relationship.

When you meet for the first time (whether virtually or in-person) you should have plenty to discuss. As you begin to share information, you will **Embark, Observe**, and **Discover**. These three steps are important, and moving through these steps could take several meetings occurring over weeks or even months. Resist the temptation to move hastily through the steps. Remember, this is a journey, not a race. Spending time in these areas could pay big dividends. If you are a mentee, you might find that the goal you were hoping to reach isn't really the right goal for you after all. If you are the mentor, you might learn something about the mentee that prompts you to recall relevant experiences that may have laid dormant in your subconscious for some time. So, be generous when revealing information about yourself and your aspirations, as the conversations will lay the foundation for a relationship built on candor and trust.

When the time is right, you'll be ready to **Map** and **Survey**. At this point, you'll lock into goals for the partnership, and will develop a plan to arrive at the desired outcomes. You may discuss resources, identify next steps, and seek or provide direction.

If the mentoring process were linear, we might have developed a straight-line model with directional arrows. But, it's not. As with many journeys, you may encounter a few pot holes or be tempted by a diversion along the way. Unexpected events, positive or negative, may cause you to revert back to Map to reexamine your goals, or retreat to Explore to reconsider your skills and strengths.

Since every mentoring experience is different, it's difficult to predict how long you will remain in any phase, and it's difficult to know how long it might take to achieve your collective goals. What we do know is that, at some point, the relationship may come to a purposeful end, may dissolve or may morph into a different relationship with different goals. Some mentoring relationships will last only a short time, while others may change shape and may extend over many years.

Getting the Most from This Book

We wrote *The Career Compass* for both the mentor and the mentee. By our definition, the mentee drives the relationship, asking for what they need in the context of their goals. The mentor helps to structure the relationship by holding the mentee accountable, pushing them beyond their comfort zone, and providing tough feedback when needed.

The book is, therefore, designed to benefit both parties, and is divided into two parts, each offering a unique perspective on a key topic. Since we believe that a disciplined approach to mentoring leads to better outcomes, we also believe that structure is critical. Since the mentor determines the structure of the relationship, we address the mentor's journey first.

If you plan to be a mentor, you'll want to read the first half of this book. If you are hoping to find a mentor, you'll want to read the second half. If your goal is to learn as much as you can about mentoring, we'd suggest reading the book from start to finish.

The Power of Mentoring

On the pages that follow, you will learn what it takes to be a good mentor, and what it takes to be a good mentee. You'll also learn how to apply the seven-step Mentoring Journey, a process that can help you forge beneficial and enduring mentoring relationships.

Whether you are searching for a mentor, or would like to mentor someone else, there is no better time than today to begin your journey. No matter what your age, stage in life, employment situation, geographic location, education level, or gender, you can benefit from having a mentor, being a mentor, or both. It is our hope that *The Career Compass* will become your go-to guide to professional and personal growth.

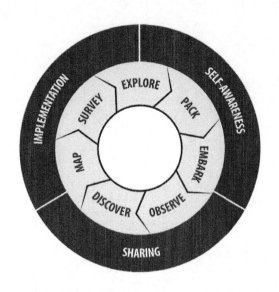

Part 1

FOR THE MENTOR

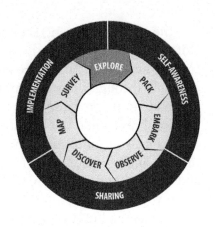

Chapter 1

EXPLORE: INTROSPECTION

*"A mentor is someone who allows you
to see the hope inside yourself."*
–Oprah Winfrey

Are You Ready to Be a Mentor?

Mentees stand to benefit from the advice, counsel, feedback, guidance and networking doors that a mentor can open. By learning at the feet of a master (a mentor), a mentee can accelerate their development, enhance their reputation, and become exposed to suitable career opportunities that might not otherwise have been evident.

But what do mentors stand to gain? An experienced leader/mentor may not need career advice. They may already be well-connected within their organization. They may be intelligent and well-respected, and may already have achieved a considerable level of success. So why would a person with so much want to give their time to others? For many, it's about the satisfaction derived from helping to pull someone else up, as they may have been pulled up years before. For others, it's about leaving a legacy, or passing along what they have learned to someone else who might benefit from their wisdom. In short, mentors are often motivated by the desire to impact someone else's career in a positive way. Most mentors want to make a difference.

The act of mentoring is primarily selfless. It's an act of generosity. Witnessing someone else thrive and succeed with your help can be extremely gratifying. But before you offer to be added to a list of mentors available through your organization's formal mentoring program, or volunteer to mentor a specific individual, take a step back. Mentoring relationships should not be entered into lightly.

Before you jump into a mentor role, we'd encourage you to take time to analyze your motives; examine your own experiences, skills and abilities; and make sure that you can realistically support a mentee given your current responsibilities and commitments. You may want to be a mentor, but the question is, "Are you ready to be one?" If you're not sure, start by answering these questions:

- Are you clear about your motivations for mentoring?

- Are you clear about what you have to offer a mentee?

- Do you have ample time to commit to a mentee or can you adjust your priorities to allow the time you'll need?

What It Takes to Be Successful

When we began studying the art and practice of mentoring, we uncovered many stories about life-altering mentoring relationships, but we found little information about the disciplines and best practices that contributed to their success. Over the years, we've worked with thousands of mentees, mentors and master mentors. We've observed patterns in their skills, abilities and behaviors, and have made a conscious effort to examine the impact of those attitudes and aptitudes on their relationships.

Through our research, we identified the key attitudes and aptitudes that correlate with success in the role of the mentor. Attitudes are the internal drivers and inclinations that fuel a mentor's passion for helping others. Aptitudes are the natural abilities that, when employed, support maximum growth in a mentoring relationship.

Review the lists that follow. Place a check by the attitudes and aptitudes that you possess. The goal is to check the boxes that best reflect the attitudes and aptitudes that you can bring to a mentoring relationship, not necessarily to check *every* box.

Attitude	Great mentors...	✓
Integrity	know who they are and have a strong moral compass	
Respect for others	seek to understand others (viewpoints, differences)	
Empathetic	listen with their heart first, and then their mind	
Honest	provide candid feedback	
Authentic	use their personal experiences to help their mentees avoid mistakes and learn from successes	
Selfless	foster success in others	
Compassionate	care about their mentees' professional and personal progress	
Courageous	initiate conflict, when necessary, to ensure the mentee is successful	
Positive	believe that the mentee can substantially benefit from the mentoring process and enthusiastically shares these beliefs	
Emotionally Intelligent	perceive their personal emotions and are sensitive to the emotions and feelings of their mentee	

Aptitude	Great mentors...	✓
Proven track record of success	exhibit success in the area where the mentee needs support	
Provide constructive feedback	point out areas that need improvement, always focusing on the mentee's behavior	
Accessible	dedicate the time and mental energy to devote to the relationship	
Good listeners	maintain eye contact and give mentees their full attention, blocking out distractions	
Communicators	demonstrate good verbal and nonverbal communication skills (storytellers)	
Internal awareness	maintain an awareness of the developments within the organization (career tracks, special projects/assignments)	
Self-awareness	understand their own strengths and weaknesses and their impact on others	
Broad range of experiences	possess positive formal or informal experiences throughout the organization	

Strategic vision	consider where the organization is headed and more importantly, where it should be going	
Resourceful	participate in networking and understand how networking can benefit the mentee, linking internal and external resources to the mentee	

Although a mentee may enter a mentoring relationship with specific questions and goals, having a mentor who is clear about their own attitudes and aptitudes will make the mentoring process more enjoyable and effective for both parties. No one is a perfect mentor for everyone, but you are the *right* mentor for someone.

What's in It for You?

In addition to evaluating your strengths and weaknesses in preparation for providing someone else career advice and support, it's important to determine what *you* need and what you hope to gain by mentoring others. In other words, what will you get out of this?

There is no right or wrong answer here, because everyone mentors for different reasons. But it is helpful to think ahead. Knowing what you want to learn and gain from the relationship can help to ensure that both you and your mentee end up winners in the end. So, answer the question…what do you want from a mentoring relationship?

- Are you interested in honing your interpersonal skills?

- Are you trying to pull yourself out of your shell?

- Are you hoping to learn something from a mentee?

- Or is there some other impetus for volunteering to mentor?

My Top 3 Goals for mentoring:

1._____

2._____

3._____

What Help Do *You* Need?

We sometimes encounter potential mentors who lack the confidence to take on the role. Some worry that they might not know enough or have the right experience to mentor others. If you find yourself in that category, don't let that deter you. If you are motivated and have something to share, then you have met the fundamental requirements for the job. That said, there may be skills that you want to develop to help you become an effective mentor.

We find that many of the best mentors have mentors of their own. Great mentors model effective behaviors and interactions, and know how to appropriately challenge their mentees. So, ask around. Do you know a mentor who could help you in the mentoring process? Can you turn to a previous mentor for advice? Having someone to emulate can help you master the craft more quickly. If you can't find a mentor, there are a lot of resources (in addition to this book) that can help you work with your mentee to develop a mentoring plan, better manage your own responsibilities to find time for mentoring, handle difficult situations or have potentially challenging conversations. Whether you turn to a seasoned veteran or rely on books and online resources for help, challenge yourself to improve your own skills so that you can be a strong support for your mentee.

Mentor Red Flags

While volunteering to serve as a mentor can be a very generous and noble act, you might not be a good candidate for mentoring, at least not right now. Think long and hard about mentoring before you jump in with both feet. Not everyone has the skills, time or motivation to help champion someone else's career. In fact, it can be difficult to find time in your own schedule to help someone else pursue their career goals. Under the right conditions, the mentoring experience can be incredibly rewarding; however, it's best not to engage with a mentee if:

- **You think you're too busy.** If you are feeling overwhelmed with current responsibilities, it's unlikely you'll be able to carve out the time required to do justice to the role. Although the time spent between a mentor and a mentee can vary by pairing, you should plan to dedicate at least one hour to mentoring per month, with no cell, text or email interruptions.

- **You routinely cancel appointments.** If you are so busy you can't squeeze in all your current commitments, it will be nearly impossible to add one more obligation to the mix, and not be tempted to cancel appointments with your mentee. Your mentee really needs you to be available on a regular basis.

- **You are not a volunteer, you are a "volun-told."** Formal mentoring programs are a great tool for organizations, but if any party – the mentor or the mentee – isn't willing and enthusiastic, the relationship will likely fall apart, and participation in the program will not yield significant results. If you're tempted to become a mentor simply because someone told you to, you may want to reconsider. If your heart isn't in it, then mentoring isn't worth your time, and it certainly won't benefit your mentee.

- **You see mentoring as a way to earn recognition.** If you are a good mentor, you will likely earn gratitude and recognition from your mentee, but you can't always expect the same from your employer. Don't count on your role as mentor to earn you anything more than self-satisfaction and mentee appreciation. If recognition is your primary reason for participating, it's best to back out now.

- **You are looking forward to the chance to talk about how great you are.** While talking about your background, career path, and successes will likely be one way to help your mentee develop a career plan, don't become a mentor so you can boast about your accomplishments. The details of your latest feat of brilliance may be viewed as pompous, unless it's used as an example to help someone else find their own path or solution. Don't go there.

- **You are not aware of your own strengths.** Since becoming a mentor involves devoting time and attention to helping someone else achieve their goals, you should be clear about your own talents and areas of development. If you can't clearly communicate your own interests, openly share your experiences, and describe how your skills and abilities helped you be successful, you may be challenged when encouraging your mentee to do the same.

Time, interest, generosity and self-confidence are keys to successful mentoring. Without these characteristics, you may not be able to meet your mentee's needs. But if your heart is truly committed to sharing what you know, then move ahead. Find a mentee who will benefit from your knowledge, attention and advice, and then follow through.

Self-Assessment

Self-awareness is a key contributor to a successful mentoring relationship. If you want to move beyond understanding your aptitudes and attitudes, a self-assessment can help you:

- Recognize your strengths and weaknesses and examine their impact on your career path, so you can better counsel your mentee

- Examine the personality quirks and mannerisms which could interfere with, or enhance, communication with your mentee

- Recall the challenges you faced while reaching your own career goals and remind yourself of lessons learned that you may want to share

- Identify areas that you need to work on that could impede your mentoring efforts

- Reflect on the paths that you took that might also benefit your mentee, as well as the paths that your mentee might want to avoid

- Confirm that you are, in fact, ready to be a mentor

Taking time to reflect on the skills that helped you reach your own career goals could make it easier to guide a mentee as they examine their own skills. Understanding how you have benefited from mentors in your life might help you determine which information to share with your mentee, and which information to keep to yourself. Revisiting pivotal career decisions (good and bad) can help you prepare for career discussions with your mentee.

The bottom line is, the more you know about yourself, the better prepared you'll be when helping your mentee.

We designed the Mentor Self-Assessment to help you examine and evaluate the benefits you can bring to a mentee, and to help you consider goals for the mentoring relationship. You can complete it independently or seek input from others.

MENTORING IN ACTION

"Mentoring is part of who I am. People call me for advice every day, and I am happy to give it. I've been fortunate to have some amazing advisors in my life. So, it's important to me to pay it forward." says Karen Finn.

Karen is the Director of Operations for a fast-growing regional freight company, and a natural-born mentor. When the company began to expand about 5 years ago, Karen saw the need to develop people, particularly those who might be well-suited for leadership positions. She met with the Executive Team and proposed a development plan for emerging leaders, which included a formal mentoring program.

As a result of her efforts, mentors from all levels of the organization are now matched with mentees who have interest in, and the ability to move into, leadership roles. Karen has found that connecting with mentees (either formally or informally) and helping them on their career paths has been one of her most rewarding accomplishments.

Karen notes that new mentees generally fall into one of two categories: 1) they either overstate their capabilities and/or underappreciate the work and experience it takes to become a successful leader, or 2) they highlight their weaknesses and inadvertently create their own barriers to promotion. Although it's important for the mentors in Karen's company to help their mentees set attainable goals and create realistic plans to achieve them, initial meetings often focus on helping high-potentials identify their strengths and link them to viable career options. Once they understand their strengths, they can move to discussions about potential gaps and opportunities for growth.

Karen says, "There was a time when, although I was relatively successful, I was unaware of my own strengths. A mentor suggested that I list each of my achievements, and identify the talents and abilities that helped me accomplish them. By completing the exercise, I learned a lot about myself. I also saw themes that ran through many of my accomplishments. My mentor encouraged me to be aware of my weaknesses, *but* to focus on my strengths. It's the best advice I've ever received.

I believe that the most successful mentors are those who have a clear understanding of their strengths, talents, and skills. By understanding my own gifts, I'm better prepared to help my mentees realize how to leverage theirs."

MENTOR SELF-ASSESSMENT

What Are Your Talents?

Check the boxes next to the talents that you can bring to a mentoring relationship.

Talents Checklist

- ❏ Adaptability
- ❏ Analysis
- ❏ Coaching
- ❏ Counseling
- ❏ Command presence
- ❏ Communication
- ❏ Creativity
- ❏ People development
- ❏ Empathy
- ❏ Empowering others
- ❏ Flexible thinking
- ❏ Influencing others
- ❏ Initiative
- ❏ Leadership
- ❏ Listening

- ❏ Managing conflict
- ❏ Managing people
- ❏ Motivating others
- ❏ Negotiating
- ❏ Networking
- ❏ Problem solving
- ❏ Self-promotion
- ❏ Strategy
- ❏ Team dynamics
- ❏ Vision
- ❏ Other:
- ❏ Other:
- ❏ Other:
- ❏ Other:
- ❏ Other:

List your Top 5 Talents below:

1._____

2._____

3._____

4._____

5._____

What Are Your Skills?

Check the boxes next to the skills that you can bring to a mentoring relationship.

Skills Checklist

- ❏ Administrative skills
- ❏ Analytics
- ❏ Budgeting
- ❏ Business development
- ❏ Business solutions
- ❏ Career planning
- ❏ Computer skills
- ❏ Cost management
- ❏ Decision making
- ❏ Interpersonal skills
- ❏ Interviewing skills
- ❏ Market development
- ❏ Marketing skills
- ❏ Organizing and planning

- ❏ Prioritizing
- ❏ Presentation skills
- ❏ Project management
- ❏ Recruiting
- ❏ Technology
- ❏ Time management
- ❏ Training
- ❏ Writing skills
- ❏ Other:
- ❏ Other:
- ❏ Other:
- ❏ Other:
- ❏ Other:
- ❏ Other:

List your Top 5 Skills below:

1._____

2._____

3._____

4._____

5._____

Reflections

Analyze and reflect on your talents and skills by answering the questions below.

1. Which talents have contributed most to your success?

   _____

   _____

   _____

2. How will your talents help you when mentoring?

   _____

   _____

   _____

3. Which skills have contributed most to your success?

   _____

   _____

   _____

4. How will your skills help you when mentoring?

   _____

   _____

   _____

6. What career experiences have been most beneficial to your professional development?

   _____

   _____

   _____

7. What did you learn from those experiences?

_____

_____

_____

Past Mentoring Experience

Reflect on a past mentoring experience when answering the questions below.

1. What was the single most important piece of advice you received from your mentor?

_____

_____

_____

2. How did your mentor empower you to be more successful?

_____

_____

_____

3. How did your mentor affect your personal or professional development?

_____

_____

_____

4. How have mentors helped you in the past?

_____

_____

_____

5. How can your talents, skills and experiences benefit a mentee?

_____

_____

_____

6. What personal experiences do you hope to share?

_____

_____

_____

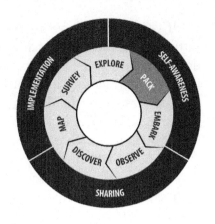

Chapter 2

PACK: GATHER INFORMATION

"A lot of people have gone farther than they thought they could because someone else thought they could."
—Unknown

Getting Started

Once you make the decision to become a mentor the next step should be easy, if your employer has a formal mentoring program in place. Mentoring initiatives are often supported through Human Resource departments or leadership development groups, so start there. You might simply need to fill out a form and volunteer to be added to the mentor database. With the tap of a few keys, you could be matched with potential mentees.

However, if your organization lacks a formal mentoring process, it doesn't mean that there aren't opportunities for mentoring. It just might mean that you may have to work a little harder to find the right mentee. In the absence of a formal program, you can: 1) identify someone you would like to mentor, 2) wait until someone approaches you directly (which doesn't happen very often), or 3) let others know that you would like to be a mentor and are in search of a mentee. If you get the word out, odds are pretty good you'll find a mentee who is eager to learn from your advice.

If you want to have an even greater impact, you might consider setting up a mentor matching process within your department. It doesn't need to be complex. A simple structure could provide a way for potential mentors to volunteer to help potential mentees grow in their careers, understand or embrace the corporate culture, or navigate the political landscape.

If you don't have the time or interest to spearhead the creation of an entirely new mentoring program, how about simply volunteering to help new employees? Speak to your manager, visit your human resources department, and spread the word among your colleagues. Let them know that you would be happy to sit down with new hires and share some words of wisdom for succeeding within your organization. Who knows, through these meetings, you just might find the right mentee.

Although your place of employment is a good place to start, don't hesitate to expand your search. You might find your "perfect" mentee within an association or group to which you belong. Formal mentoring programs are becoming more popular with professional and networking organizations, as they expand benefits to attract and engage their members. Some groups match industry veterans with those new to the field, others open their programs to match experienced mentors with mentees based on their individual goals. For example, an individual displaced by a merger might be looking for help finding focus and defining the activities and steps that will lead them to their next role. Or they may be looking for a mentor who has switched careers within their industry. Another individual might be trying to figure out what's next for them on the career ladder. They may be looking for a mentor who transitioned from sales to marketing, for example. Or there might be a potential mentee looking to become an entrepreneur, and in search of a mentor who transitioned from the corporate world to their own business.

Alternatively, you could take a wait-and-see approach, remaining open to a mentoring relationship when the opportunity is right. This is the preferred approach for many potential mentors who do not have the time to actively pursue an appropriate mentee. Rest assured, if you are open, a mentee will enter into your life at just the right time.

Success Breeds Success

While you will no doubt be looking for a qualified mentee who fits your personality and style, be aware that individuals who have distinguished themselves in some way – demonstrating considerable talent, ambition or early success – are the most common candidates. Bright, ambitious employees often have the self-confidence to ask for guidance and counsel. Struggling employees with lower levels of confidence may be less assertive and less likely to seek a mentor. Mentees who have already achieved some degree of achievement are likely to continue along that path to success, which is why they are often obvious candidates for mentoring. That's not to say, though, that you should rule out candidates with marginal performance, or new hires lacking a track record. It's possible that the individuals simply haven't yet shown their talents. With a little effort, you may find a star in the making. But be selective. Your mentee's reputation and track record could reflect on you.

Evaluating Potential Mentees

If you completed the Self-Assessment in Chapter 1, you likely have a good sense of what mentees can learn from you, and understand who might benefit the most from your guidance and direction. You can use your insights to develop a profile of your perfect potential mentee.

To develop a profile, answer the questions below:

- What is your mentee's current position?

- Where do they work (business unit or functional area)?

- What is their level of education?

- How long has the person been with the organization or been pursuing their dream role?

- What are their career aspirations?

- What are their goals?

- What are their skills?

- What are their social circles?

- What are their personal interests?

By answering these questions you'll develop a list of characteristics that can help you spot potential mentees. Deciding that your ideal mentee will already have an MBA, for example, could lead you to groups or individuals who fall into that category. If you're looking for a mentee in a particular functional area, you could check with local colleges and universities to find recent grads in need of guidance, or with local chapters of national professional associations and societies. Don't limit the scope of your search. Cast a wide net. There are likely many candidates who will fit your profile, or at least meet many of the criteria. Remain flexible and open-minded in your search, and the odds of finding a terrific mentee will increase significantly.

Matching Goals and Objectives

Once you've identified a potential mentee who could benefit from your experiences and insights, you'll want to understand the individual's goals for mentoring to make sure that you are well-aligned. For example, if your goal is to help retain talent at your current employer, an individual trying to network themselves into a job at another company might not be a good fit.

Likewise, if your goal is to help a mentee rise quickly through the organization, a candidate in need of advice about how to overcome a series of recent missteps in their current role might not be a good fit. Make sure you're on the same page and path before you make a commitment to a mentee. Misaligned goals can result in little progress, and a great deal of frustration.

Questions you may want to ask potential mentees include:

- Why do you want to be mentored?

- How do you want to be mentored – in person, by phone or by email?

- What are your goals for a mentoring relationship?

- Can you describe some of your recent accomplishments? What lessons have you learned from recent missteps or failures?

- Have you ever worked with a mentor?

o   How well did the relationship work?
o   What did you learn from your mentor?
o   What would have improved the experience?

- What do you hope to gain from this mentoring relationship?

Once you've had a discussion with a potential mentee, you should clearly understand their goals and expectations. Take some time to reflect on the information you collected:

- Do you think the mentee truly wants mentoring and career guidance, or is the person more interested in tapping into your network?

- Can you trust the mentee? (For example, would you be comfortable sharing sensitive information about the company and/ or your past failures to help them make progress?)

- Are the mentee's goals realistic given their track record?

- Does the mentee appear open to constructive criticism?

- Are you confident you can provide feedback in a way that will motivate the mentee to take action?

- Is the individual likely to take the action required to make progress?

- Are you the best mentor to help the individual achieve their goals?

- How well do the mentee's goals align with your own?

If you are an intuitive person, trust your instincts. What does your gut tell you? Are you excited about helping the prospective mentee reach their full potential? Do you see how your past experience and their current career path are parallel in some respects, or are you sensing that ego may get in the way of your being able to assist and redirect the person's efforts? Both of you should be excited about the progress you can make together.

Do Your Homework

Even after you've had a discussion with a potential mentee, you might feel that you're lacking sufficient information to determine whether this could be a fruitful relationship or a frustrating alliance. Before you commit, take time to learn more about your prospective candidate. Many people maintain an online presence. You might learn from a quick search of the internet, but always let your prospective mentee know about your research. Being transparent from the start will help to build a trusting relationship.

When gathering information online, try the following sites or apps:

- Google – A Google search may help you learn about an individual's interests and accolades.

- LinkedIn – This professional networking website allows you to review online profiles and check in with people who may have worked with your prospective mentee at previous employers.

- Facebook – Part business tool and part personal communication device, Facebook may reveal a lot about a person.

- Instagram – This tool allows for photo and video sharing and can reveal information similar to Facebook.

- Twitter – Twitter is another communication tool that can give you a snapshot of what your mentee candidate routinely talks about online.

- YouTube – This site offers the ability to share videos, and may give you a glimpse into your candidate's interests.

Understanding Your Role

As you move forward in selecting a mentee and designing a regular schedule of contact, be sure that you are ready for your new responsibilities. Mentoring is different from supervising or managing in a number of important ways. Strong mentors:

- Commit to regular meetings with their mentees, adjusting their schedules to align with their mentee's availability

- Communicate openly about their successes and failures, so the mentee can model similar behavior or learn from their mentor's mistakes

- Coach the mentee regarding weaknesses or skill sets that need to be developed, without judgment or discouragement

- Champion the reputation of their mentee by helping them find new and challenging assignments

- Offer guidance and observation without trying to control or manipulate the mentee's decisions or actions

- Provide professional and emotional support when things do not go as planned for the mentee

MENTORING IN ACTION

Alexis Chen mentors dozens of professional men and women simultaneously at any given time. She takes the role seriously, and is committed to offering her mentees the same benefits she received from those who have mentored her over the years. She wants to help her mentees recognize and label their talents and build their confidence, and – when appropriate – she is prepared to offer candid insights and feedback to help them grow and succeed.

Alexis says that mentees typically ask for advice related to moving into leadership roles, gaining additional breadth of experience through a lateral move, continuing to grow and develop in their current position, or making a drastic career change. "As a Mentor, I feel that it's my responsibility to understand the opportunities that would align best with my mentee's talents and aspirations," she says. "But, honestly, I don't agree to mentor every person who asks. In fact, I'm pretty selective. I don't have the time or the energy to mentor people who aren't in it for the right reasons, and who aren't likely to be successful."

Alexis looks for mentees who:

- Are enthusiastic about mentoring and have the desire to grow and develop.
- Have clear goals and objectives for the mentoring relationship.
- Are willing and able to maintain confidential information.
- Are able to accept feedback and act on it.
- Understand and believe their mentor has their best interests at heart.
- Are comfortable driving the communication and owning the mentoring relationship.

Mentoring has provided Alexis with many opportunities to give back by sharing the knowledge she has gained through years of experience. But, she says, "I would argue that in many relationships, mentors derive greater benefits from mentoring than their mentees."

MENTOR'S PACKING LIST

When planning for a trip, a packing list can help to make sure you are prepared to travel. Likewise, the Mentor's Packing List can help you prepare to interview potential mentees.

Part 1: Planning and Preparation

Who is your ideal mentee? Summarize your Mentee's Profile here:

_____

_____

_____

_____

_____

_____

_____

_____

What is your plan for finding the right mentee? What questions will you ask a potential mentee? (Check all that apply)

- ❏ Why do you want to be mentored?
- ❏ How do you want to be mentored – in person, by phone or by email?
- ❏ What are your goals for a mentoring relationship?
- ❏ What are some recent examples of successes you've had?
- ❏ What lessons have you learned from recent missteps or failures?
- ❏ Have you ever worked with a mentor? What did you learn from your mentor?
- ❏ What do you hope to gain from this mentoring relationship?

Part 2: Reflection

(Complete this section following an initial meeting with a potential mentee.)

I learned that...

_____

_____

_____

_____

_____

I can help by...

_____

_____

_____

_____

_____

My choice for a mentee is:

_____

_____

I think they are a good fit because...

_____

_____

_____

_____

_____

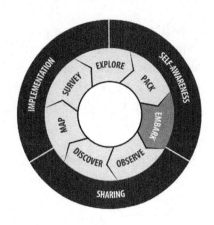

Chapter 3

EMBARK: LAY THE FOUNDATION

"One of the things I keep learning is that the secret of being happy is doing things for other people."
—Dick Gregory

Taking the First Step

The initial meeting with your mentee will set the tone for the mentoring relationship. It's ideal to have that meeting in person, but that might not be possible, particularly if the mentoring relationship spans the country or the globe. Regardless, you will want the conversation to include more than simple pleasantries and idle chatter. Think of your first connection like a first date. You'll want to make a good impression, act appropriately, listen carefully for clues about your mentee's personality and perspective, and share useful information so your mentee will want to talk again. Recognize that, as the mentor, you're the host. That means that – at least for this initial meeting – you'll lead the discussion, propose an agenda, and assume responsibility for making sure your mentee derives value from the interaction, and you will determine how long the first meeting should last.

A typical first meeting can average an hour to an hour-and-a-half, but there is no hard and fast rule. Just make sure to allow ample time to learn about each other, establish clear expectations for the relationship, and develop a plan to get the mentorship started. The more comfortable your mentee is, the more they may be willing to share about their background, goals, strengths, weaknesses, successes and failures. However, don't feel obligated to stretch the meeting out, if you accomplish what you need to in 45 minutes.

Preparing for the Discussion

As the meeting host, you'll want to show up prepared and ready to share. Prior to the meeting, you should review your mentee's resume and any additional information they may have provided. Look for hints that could point to the individual's true passion. Identify areas where your mentee may struggle. With permission, reach out to others to learn about your mentee's strengths and weaknesses, or check in with a previous manager to learn more about your protégé.

You'll also want to be ready to make assignments and recommend resources to help your mentee get started on their mentoring journey. It can be easier to identify resources if you are clear about your mentee's aspirations, but even if you aren't, you can still recommend books, websites, associations, and other sources the mentee might turn to for information and inspiration.

In addition, you may want to take a few minutes to review the Mentor Self-Assessment that you completed in Chapter 1. Reflect on your strengths. Think about the ways in which you could assist a mentee. Also, take a few moments to review your list of contacts. Are there others you respect who might be in a position to help a mentee whose interests or needs fall outside your areas of expertise? Finally, check your calendar; be prepared to compare schedules to find available dates for future meetings.

Getting Comfortable

Keep in mind that your mentee might be nervous about your first one-on-one meeting. They may worry that they could say the wrong thing. They may fear that they are unprepared or unworthy. Although you, too, might be nervous, it's your job to help the mentee feel at ease.

Consider this when selecting a venue. If possible, pick a place and time that puts you both at ease. You might head to a coffee shop, take a walk through a park, or sit at a quiet table at a local restaurant. If meeting outside the workplace isn't an option, try to find a space where you can minimize interruptions. If you decide to meet in your office, pull your chair out from behind the desk, or sit at a small table. Remember: this is a collaborative meeting, not a negotiation. Wherever you go, keep the discussion light, smile, and invite conversation.

Before your mentee arrives for the meeting, turn off your cell phone and computer. Remove as many distractions as possible so you can dedicate your time and attention to the conversation.

Watch for Clues

As you begin the meeting, be aware of nonverbal clues and indications that your mentee may be nervous or uncomfortable when discussing certain topics. In particular, watch for:

- Arms crossed in front. People often do this instinctively when they are upset or fearful. It could be symptomatic of a fight or flight response. However, it doesn't necessarily mean the person is angry, perhaps they are just wary or anxious.

- Lack of eye contact. Lack of eye contact could correlate with a lack of confidence. When we are confident, we tend to look at others directly. When we lack confidence, or feel subordinate, we are more likely to avoid direct eye contact. A lack of eye contact might also indicate low self-esteem.

- Frequent head nodding. Occasional nods can indicate your mentee is actively listening and in agreement with you, but constant head nodding may mean that they have lost interest or are not paying attention.

- Leaning back in the chair. People who are interested and engaged tend to lean forward. Leaning away could indicate that an individual is bored or aloof.

- Facial expressions. Changes in expression are often easy to read, and difficult to hide. For example, raised eyebrows can indicate fatigue or frustration, while a furrowed brow might stem from confusion or annoyance.

We're not suggesting that you need to become an expert in body language, but paying attention to your mentee may help you learn more about them and their needs. If you notice any of the things we describe, make an extra effort to calm your mentee. Getting them past their nervousness and discomfort will be important to building your relationship. Not surprisingly, it can be difficult to develop a strong mentorship with someone who is fearful or uncomfortable. Honesty and transparency are critical aspects of mentoring, and they will only appear when your mentee is at ease. You can't help a mentee who isn't willing to open up enough to reveal what they truly want and need.

Establishing Trust

Trust is the firm belief in the reliability, truth, ability, or strength of someone or something, and it is an essential ingredient of any successful mentoring relationship. Trust brings down the walls between people. It supports the free flow of information, and allows for honest exchanges. It provides a basis for maximum growth. Without trust, neither the mentor nor the mentee will reach their full potential.

Although trust may not be fully developed during a single meeting, there are a few things you can do to lay a foundation for a trusting mentorship. For example, you might:

- Share something personal. When you reveal a bit of your authentic self, you will show your mentee that you are willing to be open, and may prompt your mentee to share personal information.

- Show your mentee that you care. This can be done through words or actions. Tell them how much the opportunity to mentor means to you, or block off time to help them conquer an overwhelming or important task.

- Hold true to your commitments. If you say that you will meet for an hour, arrive on time and don't cut the meeting short.

- Maintain confidentiality. Every conversation should remain in "the vault," unless there is joint agreement that the information can be shared with others who may be in a position to help.

Sharing Information

The purpose of your first meeting is for you and your mentee to get to know one another with an eye toward mapping out a plan to help your mentee achieve their goals. You can start the ball rolling by sharing some information about yourself. Your mentee may have come to the meeting with a sense of who you are and what you do, but it's always smart to make sure their information is accurate.

Be prepared to be vulnerable. Sharing personal and professional experiences can help your mentee get to know you, and can help them understand how you got from where you once were, to where you are today. Trust develops more quickly when *both* people are willing to share somewhat sensitive information. It's important for mentees to see your strengths and imperfections.

If you're not sure where to begin, you might start by talking about your career history, using your résumé as a guide. Talk about the assignments that you enjoyed the most, and the ones you didn't like at all. Share your insights. Talk about the skills that helped you be successful, and the abilities you had to develop along the way. Discuss any decisions or detours – good or bad – that led you to where you are now.

You might also reveal something you learned about yourself from the Mentor Self-Assessment. Talk about the talents and skills that you can bring to the relationship, and discuss how you might help your mentee succeed. You might also want to mention some of your weaknesses. It could put your guest at ease, and reassure them that you are human.

Don't hesitate to share something personal, if you are comfortable. For example, you might talk about your family, and how you balance your work and personal life. You might talk about a hobby, or poke fun at a habit you're known for. Consider sharing details about your upbringing, or stories about your siblings. Tell your mentee about your college years, or when you first knew you wanted to be a _____. Ultimately, talking about life outside of work will help your mentee learn more about you and better appreciate your advice.

Turning the Tables

Once you've set the stage, encourage your mentee to share. You can use your mentee's résumé to prompt conversation. When your mentee talks about their career, you'll learn about their motivations, priorities and other important factors that affected the choices made along the way.

There is a Mentee Self-Assessment at the end of chapter 10. Encourage your mentee to complete it before the meeting, and you will have even more to talk about. If your mentee is comfortable, you can review the results of the Self-Assessment together.

Always ask about the individual's goals and objectives, and find out how your mentee thinks you can help. What are the person's strengths? What skills will they need to develop? Find out if your mentee is facing political challenges or dealing with barriers that are challenging to overcome. Does the individual need advice regarding how to approach a dilemma or solve a problem? You can learn by asking questions, and can provide value by offering solutions.

Learning about the person you agreed to mentor will help you determine how you can collaborate to tackle their obstacles and achieve their goals, but you may not necessarily align when it comes to your perspectives on your mentee's challenges and weaknesses. For example, your mentee may find a certain roadblock insurmountable, while – from your perspective – it may be an insignificant bump in the road. Or your mentee may view initiative as a strength, while you know that unbridled ambition could be misinterpreted. You'll need to be tactful when sharing your perspective, so as not to belittle your mentee's concerns. As you get to know your mentee, it should become easier to provide constructive feedback that will be well received.

The Mentoring Rule Book

All relationships have dos and don'ts. Romantic relationships contain unwritten rules about proper behavior and expectations. Employee handbooks clarify expectations for the employee and the employer. Mentoring relationships are no different. Clear expectations and stated guidelines can establish how the relationship will function and avoid misunderstandings. Although you and your mentee will want to decide what is realistic and appropriate, the following are common mentoring guidelines to discuss and consider:

- Commit to meeting on a regular basis

- Start and end each meeting on time

- Put interruptions aside so you can make full use of your time together

- Communicate openly about successes and failures

- Provide timely and candid feedback (be honest, yet tactful)

- Clarify responsibilities

- Keep all commitments

- Keep all conversations confidential

- Work through minor concerns

- Continuously evaluate the relationship

- Honor each other's expertise and experience

- Work together to the best of your ability for the agreed-upon duration of the mentorship

Depending on your work styles and preferences, you may decide to add expectations to the list above, or you may elect to remove items from the proposed list. The important part is reviewing and discussing how the relationship will work in an effort to eliminate damaging surprises for either party down the road. Setting guiding principles also demonstrates to your mentee how seriously you take your time together, and reinforces your commitment to their growth and success.

Setting Expectations and Developing a Plan

As you discuss the mentoring process and make agreements about how you will work together, ask your mentee to share their expectations for the next 12 months (or for the duration of the mentorship). Are their goals realistic and attainable? You may find that you need to reign in expectations. For example, your mentee will not be guaranteed a promotion simply because you are their mentor. And if your mentee is expecting to tag along to executive committee meetings, you might need to reset expectations.

Perhaps your mentee's goals *are* realistic and attainable, just not in 12 months. If that's the case, you might want to help them design a 24-month or 36-month plan, and then identify ways that you can help during the period of the mentorship. Figure out where your mentee can expect to be after a year of your guidance, and let them know that you will help them plan from there.

Once you've confirmed realistic expectations, work with your mentee to break their overarching objective(s) into individual monthly goals that you can review at each meeting. Parsing larger goals into manageable steps will help your mentee calendar the tasks that will lead to their destination.

As the conversation winds down, remember to compare your calendars and schedule your next meeting. If possible, look ahead and confirm as many meetings as you can. Locking them in will ensure that you and your mentee make time for each other regardless of any competing priorities. Then, review each of your actions and agreements leading up to your next meeting.

Different Is Good

During your initial meeting, you may start to spot personality differences between you and your mentee, especially if you spend more than an hour together. Maybe your mentee is not quite as self-confident or outspoken as you are, or perhaps he is more so. Your mentee may be serious, where you are not, or very casual where you are ultra-professional. Differences are inevitable, and generally, that's a good thing!

Sure, you may feel a little out of your element as you counsel someone who isn't exactly like you, but that's okay. Not everyone is a carbon copy of you or your friends. Those differences offer an opportunity for you to grow and learn from your mentee's background and talents. In fact, by mentoring someone who is different from you, you will receive great benefits, because you will learn from them. By mentoring someone with different interests, you can expand your knowledge, as well as your professional and interpersonal skills.

If you are initially concerned that your differences are too significant to permit a mutually satisfying working relationship, allow yourselves a couple more meetings before making the decision to terminate the mentorship. Your initial get-together is only a starting point. Don't base your impression of a mentee on a single, solitary hour. Give the relationship some time before suggesting a change. If, after your third meeting, it is clear to you that your mentee would be better served by a different mentor, suggest someone else to take your place. Continuing to try to force a relationship that won't be satisfying to you or your mentee doesn't make sense. It's not a good use of your time and resources, and it won't benefit the mentee.

MENTORING IN ACTION

Maria Rivera is one of Andrew Stack's mentees. They were paired through their company's mentoring program. The pair met a couple of times to discuss Maria's background, experience, career aspirations and goals for mentoring. At first, Andrew was impressed. Maria seemed to have boundless energy and a passion for helping others. He was looking forward to helping her develop her potential, and thought she might be a good candidate for a leadership role. But the mentorship didn't get off to the quick start Andrew had hoped for.

During their first few months together, Maria seemed overwhelmed by day-to-day tasks. She regularly contacted Andrew to discuss what he thought were trivial annoyances. He had hoped that he and Maria would work on more strategic pursuits, and was tiring of the constant interruptions about things that weren't aligned with their mentoring objectives. Although Andrew really wanted to help Maria, he knew that something had to change, if the relationship were going to work for either of them.

To try to get the partnership on track, Andrew created a list of expectations for the mentoring relationship to share with Maria. The next time they met, Andrew shared his concerns. He reminded Maria of the goals she had for mentoring and helped her to see why those goals would be impossible to achieve if they continued on the current path. It was a breakthrough for the pair, and an enlightening moment for Maria. The two agreed to meet for coffee once a month. Between scheduled meetings, Maria would capture routine questions and concerns in her mentoring journal.

Maria found that by the time the meeting rolled around, most of her questions had been answered and concerns resolved, which left the pair with ample time to work on more important topics that advanced Maria's goals.

As a result of his mentoring experience with Maria, reviewing expectations is now part of Andrew's initial meetings with all of his mentees. He says, "Reviewing expectations early in the relationship is a necessary component to mentoring success."

EMBARK ON THE MENTORING JOURNEY

Complete this worksheet following the initial meeting with your mentee.

Part 1: The Initial Meeting
My mentee appeared…
(Ex. comfortable, uncomfortable, excited, hopeful, fearful, etc.)

_____

_____

_____

_____

We talked about…

_____

_____

_____

_____

I learned that my mentee…

_____

_____

_____

_____

Rules for the mentorship:

_____

_____

_____

_____

Part 2: Goals for Mentoring

We agreed to work together for _____ months from __/__/__ to __/__/__.

My mentee's overarching objective is:

_____

_____

_____

Monthly Goals		
Month	Goal	Scheduled Meetings

Additional insights and observations:

_____

_____

_____

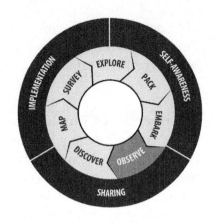

Chapter 4

OBSERVE: TUNE IN

"Unless we think of others and do something for them, we miss one of the greatest sources of happiness."
—Ray Lyman Wilbur

As you meet with your mentee, you'll learn about their background and personal interests, progress toward their stated career goals, and the stumbling blocks they encounter along the way. You'll also find ways to aid in their development and contribute to their ultimate success.

This stage, Observe, is surprisingly more important for you than it is for your mentee. During this time, you'll gather the information you need to be an effective mentor. The best way to zero in on who your mentee is, and what they need, is through active listening. Early in the relationship, it's more important to listen than to make quick recommendations. The observations you will make during your meetings, and the insights you will gain, will be critical for your mentee to hear at some point. It's important to listen carefully to what your mentee says – and doesn't say – about their professional life. So, bite your tongue for a bit, and keep your ears and eyes open. This will allow you to provide discerning recommendations during future meetings. General feedback pales in comparison to on-target assessments and laser-focused evaluations related to your mentee's unique challenges and opportunities. So, invest the time you need to get to know who your mentee *really* is, and examine paths that might help them achieve both success and satisfaction.

The Benefits of Journals

As you're listening intently to what your mentee has to say, it's a good idea to take notes. (With permission, of course.) We all have busy lives. It can be easy to forget the specifics of a discussion that may not seem important at the time, but could be valuable upon reflection. Maintaining a journal will help you and your mentee keep track of the details of your conversations.

If you document your interactions, you'll be able to review your notes from previous meetings in preparation for an upcoming meeting. A journal provides a place to jot down observations you've made, as well as comments from your mentee. If you are keeping a journal, you might record:

- Comments you'd like to explore in more detail at a later meeting

- Statements you may want to challenge, including potentially faulty assumptions

- Background information about past positions

- Information about previous managers and/or colleagues

- Details about roles, responsibilities and assignments

- Information regarding performance appraisals

- Explanations given for failures

- Beliefs about how success was achieved

- Names of others who have supported and championed your mentee

- Ideas for overcoming challenges

- Goals, tasks and milestones

- Resources that may help your mentee achieve their goals

- Lessons learned

By taking notes, you'll demonstrate to your mentee that you value what they have to say. Over time, you may use your notes to show progress, identify patterns, and provide evidence to support feedback that may help your mentee push beyond their self-imposed limits and challenge their thinking.

Alternatively, you could record your discussions electronically. This could be helpful for a mentee who may want to reflect on the conversation at a later time. But remain vigilant with confidentiality; you wouldn't want a recording to get into the wrong hands. Any conversation can be taken out of context. If your mentee asks if they can record your session, respond in a way that makes you comfortable.

Probing for Answers

If you truly want to "Observe and Tune In," you may have to dig deep with your questions. Unless your mentee is extremely extroverted and forthcoming with the details of their life and career, it's likely you'll need to lead the discussion. To understand the person's motivations, you might ask about their childhood and family life. For a peek into their attitudes and beliefs, you may inquire about their early role models. If your mentee is at a loss for words, telling stories about your own life may help your mentee become comfortable discussing their own experiences, interests and strengths. You'll want to draw on your best communication techniques to get them talking.

Although you can take the discussion in many directions, it's helpful to consider a starting point for conversation. During your initial meetings, you may want to help your mentee find the right path to achieving their true goals and objectives, you might want to uncover the assumptions and beliefs that may be supporting or standing in the way of their success, or you might want to learn about your mentee's career history, especially the people who have helped them along the way.

We've listed some topics and related questions to get you started.

Find the right path. If you are curious about whether your mentee is on the right path, it can be helpful to start with general questions, and then hone in on specific aspects of their life as you learn more about your mentee. You might ask:

- Where did you grow up?

- What did your parents do?

- Do you have brothers or sisters?

- How did you like to spend your time as a child or young adult?

- Tell me about your education.

- Where did you go to school?

- What were your favorite subjects?

- What did you like most/least about your school?

- Were you strong in sports or the arts or some other extracurricular activity?

- What characteristics do you look for in friends?

- Where else have you worked?

- How did you end up at your current employer?

- Can you recall a job that you didn't like?

- How do you like to spend your spare time?

- If you could do anything, what would you do?

Uncover assumptions and beliefs. Sometimes assumptions and/or long-held beliefs can hold people back and prevent them from act-ing on their aspirations. Have you ever heard the saying, "If you believe something is impossible, then it is"? Lots of things can get in the way of achieving a goal. As a mentor, it's your job to find out what might be standing in the way of your mentee's success. So, ask questions to unearth the assumptions that might be affecting your mentee's path. Your questions could include:

- How did you decide which college or university to attend?

- How did you pick your major?

- What drew you to your current employer?

- Why did you accept your current position?

- What prevented you from applying for the job you really wanted?

- When you had multiple options or job offers, how did you choose?

- What position are you aiming for? Why aren't you in that position now?

- What is your ultimate career goal?

- What is holding you back?

- What skills and abilities are you lacking?

- Who can help you?

- Who do you admire? Why?

Gather background information about past positions. Learning about your mentee's previous positions can be useful when brainstorming potential future roles, projects or paths. One does not have to climb a ladder to progress through a career; a lateral move may be what's needed to help strengthen identified weaknesses or gain necessary experience. By asking questions, you can learn about your mentee's likes and dislikes and help them compare their preferences with the expectations associated with the position they hope to obtain. Are they well aligned? To find out, you can start with questions like these:

- Why do you think you were offered your first job when there were other equally talented candidates?

- What did you do particularly well at that job?

- Was there anything you didn't like about the position?

- Why did you decide to leave that position?

- What was appealing about your next job that made it more interesting than the last job?

- Was it as positive an experience as you had hoped?

- What would have made it more satisfying?

- Describe your perfect job.

- How is it different from the job you hold now?

Talk about past managers. While your mentee's skills, abilities and motivations may determine how well they might fare in a particular position, the person's manager or supervisor can also play a critical role. Ask questions like those below to help identify characteristics of a manager under which your mentee can flourish:

- Who was the best manager you ever had?

- Why do you consider this individual to be your best manager?

- What did this manager make possible for you?

- What observations and advice did you find most helpful?

- Did this individual provide training or guidance?

- Which of your manager's strengths have you tried to emulate?

- Were your personalities similar or different?

- Did your manager help you network with others in the company?

- What was your worst manager like?

- How was your worst manager different from your best manager?

- What could this person have done differently to be a more positive influence?

- What type of feedback have you received from previous managers?

- Did you agree or disagree with their advice?

- Did their feedback or advice influence you in any way? If so, how?

Learn about current roles, responsibilities and assignments. Every mentee with a job shoulders a laundry list of responsibilities. Your mentee's attitudes toward their current and past assignments could support, or interfere with, their career progression. You will want to scratch below the surface to learn more about their perspectives and motivations:

- What were the roles and responsibilities with each of your past jobs?

- Did your responsibilities change or increase as you moved from one position to the next?

- Did you ever take on responsibilities above and beyond what your job title called for? Why or why not?

- Did you ever ask for additional responsibility?

- Did you receive praise or gratitude for your extra work?

- Did you ever turn down a request to tackle a specific project or task? If so, why?

- Looking back, was that a smart move?

- How did your supervisor react?

- Do you think it impacted your reputation?

- Did you ever apply for an assignment and not get it?

- What was the feedback regarding why you were not selected?

- Have you ever declined a project or job because you felt you were not qualified? Why?

- Are there specific skills you lack that you believe could have helped you in past positions?

Discuss performance appraisals. In many cases, it's clear what an individual's strengths and weaknesses are, so performance appraisals are rarely a surprise. But sometimes a mentee's perception of themselves and their skills may be quite different from their manager's evaluation. Ask these types of questions to learn more about your mentee's perception of the validity of past performance appraisals:

- What kind of performance appraisals do you generally receive?

- How have they compared with your peers?

- Have you been pleased with the appraisals you've received?

- Have you agreed with past feedback? Why or why not?

- What strengths have your managers identified?

- What areas have you been told you need to work on?

- Have you taken advice provided during performance reviews? Why or why not?

- Which assignment or job resulted in your best performance review? Why?

- Have you ever had a poor review? If so, how did you respond?

- What could you have done differently that might have improved your evaluation?

- How would you summarize your most recent performance review?

Examine explanations for failures. Although hearing that your mentee has a track record of success can be a source of optimism, exploring their failures will likely provide the insights you'll need to help them achieve a breakthrough. Try to get at the root cause of missteps that can serve as lessons for your mentee. Questions like these can help:

- Has there ever been a project or assignment where you did not achieve the results you wanted or expected?

- Why don't you think you succeeded?

- How much of the failure was your fault?

- How did others you were working with fail you?

- What could you have done to avert failure?

- Have you had any other similar experiences?

- Tell me about a failed project or effort that was totally your fault.

- What have you done to try to prevent the same situation from happening again?

- What have you learned from these failures?

- What types of projects do you think you would be likely to fail at today?

- Is there anything you can do to prevent missteps in the future?

Examine beliefs about how success was achieved. Just as dissecting failure can be a useful and informative exercise, so can a discussion about the factors that have contributed to your mentee's success. Does your mentee take sole credit for their good fortune, or are they so modest and humble that they tend to downplay their contributions? How a mentee frames their successes will tell you a lot about their level of self-confidence and their leadership potential. Ask questions like these to examine their beliefs about success:

- Tell me about a recent successful assignment.

- Why do you consider it a success?

- Would others consider it a success? Why or why not?

- To what do you attribute that success?

- Who else contributed in a significant way?

- What support did you receive?

- Were there any improvements you could have made?

- Were there any challenges you had to overcome?

- What difficulties interfered with the level of success you could have achieved?

- What did you learn from the experience that will help you on future assignments?

- Tell me about a time when you were successful because of someone else's efforts.

- Why were their contributions more important to the success of the project than yours?

- Did you recognize their contributions publicly? How?

Identify others who have supported and championed your mentee. Knowing that you have a potential posse of supporters to turn to for advice about your mentee – people who already know and like your mentee – can be both reassuring and useful. There is power in being able to tap into a team of professionals who are willing to help. To identify potential supporters, ask questions like these:

- Tell me about the people who have helped you achieve professional success.

- Do you have any role models in your current or past employer organizations?

- Would you consider your current boss one of your fans?

- Do you have other supporters?

- If I asked you to request three letters of recommendation, whom would you turn to first?

- Are there individuals who know you well in other companies?

- Are you fairly well-known within local professional organizations or trade groups? Which ones?

- Do you serve as a volunteer at any local charities? Are you actively involved?

- Has anyone been instrumental in your career thus far? Who?

- Who else might be in a position to help you?

Explore strategies for overcoming challenges. Some people are naturally solutions-oriented. When they encounter a problem or roadblock, they instinctively begin to brainstorm workarounds. But some people struggle and can become paralyzed when things don't go as planned. Is your mentee able to generate possible approaches to challenges as they emerge, or is your mentee more likely to sit back and wait for someone else to determine the next move? Is your mentee proactive or reactive? Explore your mentee's drive and problem-solving skills with questions like these:

- When given an assignment, do you follow the instructions to the letter or will you vary the approach if you think there's a better way?

- Give me an example of a time when you followed directions exactly as given. What was your rationale?

- Tell me about a time when you didn't do things exactly as instructed. How did it turn out?

- Walk me through your process for handling an unexpected situation or problem.

- How often do you turn to others for advice?

- Who do you tend to turn to for useful counsel and ideas?

- What other resources do you rely on for inspiration or guidance?

- What do you do when you see no possible solution to your situation?

Calling on Others for Help

As you listen to your mentee and capture responses to your questions, make a list of the people and/or resources you could recommend for support. These could include:

- People – within your organization or in others, including individuals in the position to which your mentee aspires

- Organizations – including professional, trade and civic

- Training – if you spot a skill that could use further development, check into relevant training and education programs

- Coaches – sometimes a one-on-one coach can be useful for tackling a specific issue or skill, such as media or personal image

- Books – if there are books you've read that you've found particularly illuminating or that could help develop your mentee, suggest them

- Websites or Apps – that provide information or useful tools to ambitious professionals

It will be virtually impossible to get through all of your questions during the initial meeting with your mentee, so focus on the most pressing questions, and use subsequent meetings to learn more. Use inquiry to learn as much as you can about your mentee. Your goal should be to find out what you need to know, so that you can provide insightful feedback and recommendations that can truly help your mentee progress. But remember, it's not an interrogation! You are trying to start a dialogue and build a relationship.

Show You're Listening

Listening makes people feel valued, respected, and interesting. Active listening involves taking in messages, interpreting information, retaining that information, and responding appropriately. If you intend to listen actively, you must make a conscious effort to truly understand your mentee. Here are some techniques to try:

- Avoid distractions by meeting in a quiet space so you can focus on the conversation with your mentee.

- Demonstrate that you are listening with confirmatory gestures, like a head nod or a simple, "Uh huh," every once in a while.

- Ask a follow-up question, when appropriate.

- Smile and use facial expressions to reflect your understanding of what has been said.

- Check your body language to be sure you're encouraging information sharing, rather than inadvertently shutting down with crossed arms and crossed legs.

- Summarize what you heard and make connections.

- Try to spend 75% of the time listening and 25% talking during the early stages of the relationship. You'll have plenty of opportunity to talk and offer guidance in later meetings.

When you think you have a clear understanding of your mentee's experience, goals, situation, and potential challenges, wrap up the meeting and confirm your next appointment. In the next session, you'll do most of the talking, while your mentee listens.

MENTORING IN ACTION

Personal development guru, Al Kline, loves mentoring others. He says, "Mentoring can be like searching for diamonds in the rough. Sometimes mentees know exactly where they want to go, what they want to do, and how they plan to get there. But often, they don't. I'm at my best when I can help a mentee find their "right" path."

But Al rarely drives the conversation. Instead, he asks a ton of questions and listens intently. His goal is to help his mentees figure out what will truly make them happy. Al has seen too many mentees chase someone else's dream or be locked into a pre-determined goal. He believes that there's no sense pursuing an ambition that will lead to a place of dissatisfaction. Instead, he encourages his mentees to examine their motivations and explore their options, which could include a deviation from the current plan.

"It's not about telling your mentee what to do," he cautions. "It's about listening to understand where your mentee wants to go, and then helping them figure out whether they can actually get there. Sometimes helping your mentee envision success might include looking at their career in a different way. As a mentor, you can't have an impact in a short amount of time, if your mentee is unclear about the ambition they want to pursue."

"Keeping a mentee in motion and moving toward their desired destination is also part of mentoring, but they have to be self-motivated. The relationship has to be about them. It can't be about what you want as mentor," he says. "What the mentor wants is immaterial."

"In my opinion, the most effective mentors initiate mentoring relationships without a personal agenda or objective. That is only possible by putting the mentee's interests first, by looking for ways to serve the mentee, and by listening to their needs rather than considering your own ego. In exchange, you become part of who the mentee is, and ultimately who they become. I always manage to learn something I can use from the people I mentor," concludes Al.

OBSERVATION GUIDE

Use Part 1 of this guide to plan your initial discussion, and Part 2 to record observations and recommendations from the meeting.

Part 1: Discussion Topics and Questions

During our initial meeting, I would like to:
(Check all that apply.)

❏ Direct my mentee to the right path.

❏ Uncover my mentee's assumptions and beliefs.

❏ Gather background information about past positions.

❏ Talk about past managers.

❏ Learn about current roles, responsibilities and assignments.

❏ Discuss performance appraisals.

❏ Examine explanations for failures.

❏ Examine beliefs about how success was achieved.

❏ Identify others who have supported and championed your mentee.

❏ Explore strategies for overcoming challenges.

I'd like to focus on the following questions:

_____

_____

_____

Others who could help my mentee reach their goals:

_____

_____

_____

_____

_____

Part 2: Insights & Observations
Initial Observations:

_____

_____

_____

_____

_____

_____

_____

Initial Recommendations:

_____

_____

_____

_____

_____

_____

_____

Topics to discuss during the next meeting:

_____

_____

_____

_____

_____

_____

_____

_____

_____

_____

_____

_____

_____

_____

_____

_____

_____

_____

_____

_____

_____

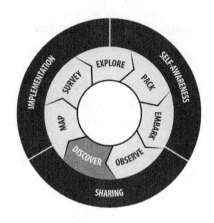

Chapter 5

DISCOVER: FEEDBACK AND ADVICE

*"If your actions inspire others to dream more, learn more, do more
and become more, you are a leader."*
—John Quincy Adams

At the initial meeting(s) with your mentee, you listened and took notes. You likely learned about your mentee's goals and aspirations, their skills and past experiences, and their hopes and expectations for the future. By this point, you may have a sense of whether your mentee's ambitions are realistic, and whether their current approach will lead them to their destination.

Now, it's time to carefully consider what you want to tell your mentee, and how you'd like to deliver the news. In some cases, it may be time for a harsh reality check, as in, "Don't quit your day job." Those conversations could be tough for both of you, but fortunately, in most cases, you won't be facing such a scenario. Rarely are mentees so totally off-base that it's difficult to determine where to begin. More often than not, your thoughts, ideas and specific feedback will be welcome, and will help put your mentee on a path to success – even if it's not the path they originally planned to take.

Easing into the Conversation

In the "Observe: Tune In" stage, the focus was on getting to know your mentee. That was an important step for *you*, because it provided much of the necessary input you needed to better understand your mentee and their objectives for the mentoring relationship. This stage, "Discover: Feedback and Advice" is critical for your mentee. At this point, you should be ready to provide objective observations, candid feedback, and well-considered guidance. Most mentees will recognize the benefit of unfiltered insights from a seasoned professional who has been where they want to go, and has achieved the level of success they are seeking. Although you might not always tell your mentee what they want to hear, in time they will come to value regular and candid dialogue from a trusted and experienced advisor.

Most conversations will be balanced, offering you the opportunity to discuss your mentee's progress, while at the same time, challenging them to think outside the box. You might have a conversation about unrecognized skills or under-utilized abilities that could help your mentee in pursuit of their goals. (Often, mentees have hidden talents just waiting to be discovered.) Or you might talk about ways to approach a new situation or challenge that has your mentee perplexed.

At this stage, your conversations will center on paying attention, and responding with feedback and advice. Keep in mind that, for some mentees, you might be their first sounding board. (The Urban Dictionary offers this definition: "A sounding board is a good listener, and either confirms what they hear or offers an opinion when what they hear is 'off key'.") So, as you did in the previous stage, listen intently to what your mentee has to say, and take good notes. Whenever possible, restate your mentee's words verbatim, without trying to summarize. For example, if your mentee states that their former boss was "controlling," use the word "controlling" rather than "micromanager" or "difficult." This will help to confirm that you heard your mentee correctly, and will allow your mentee to clarify, if needed. Repeating your mentee's statements will also help to build trust by demonstrating that you are listening intently, and that you understand what's on your mentee's mind.

If you feel your mentee is on track to achieving their short-term goals, you'll want to let them know as soon as possible. Confirmation will boost their confidence and self-esteem, and may increase their receptivity to your future recommendations. If your mentee is already on the right path, you might want to suggest things they can do to reach their goals more quickly, with an eye toward their next career stepping stone. Often, mentees take too many steps when pursuing their goals. If you reached your career aspiration by taking an alternate approach, share that with your mentee. You could save them time and limit unnecessary steps. Even if your mentee is already well-positioned for success, you can challenge them to find ways to move closer to their goals and prepare them for future positions.

Your mentee might benefit from:

- Joining a specific professional or trade organization for increased visibility and networking

- Registering for training, such as public speaking or supervising

- Volunteering for a charity supported by influential community leaders or executives

- Pursuing a leadership role on a high-visibility project

- Exploring job opportunities outside the company, or outside the country, to gain differentiated experience

- Taking advantage of the company's education allowance to earn an advanced degree or certificate

- Becoming more familiar with a new technology that is important to the company

- Agreeing to mentor a junior employee

- Improving business skills like project management, negotiating or business planning

- Studying the teachings of a respected author or consultant

- Gaining media exposure through article submissions and/or expert interviews

Opportunities for Growth

You might identify a number of opportunities for growth within your first few conversations. In fact, you may have compiled a laundry list of areas for improvement by the time a mentee has finished describing their background, experiences, and career aspirations. You may also find a disparity between what your mentee hopes to achieve short-term and their current skills. In other words, your mentee might not be ready for the promotion or position they are seeking. Whatever you do, don't start your conversation by revealing that your mentee may have unrealistic expectations. Instead, look for ways to help your mentee realize this on their own.

Leading with bad news can result in major disappointment, and could cause your mentee to shut down and shut you out completely. No one wants to hear that they are poised for failure. If you have to deliver bad news, try to balance it with something positive. You might even try using the "good news sandwich." Start by talking about something your mentee does well. Compliment them on how they handled past situations, the excellent reputation they developed, or their latest positive performance review. Then, lead in to your recommendations for improvements. Tell them where they fall short. Offer recommendations to help them advance their skills or gain needed experience. Finally, wrap it up with a positive statement about how they can leverage their talents to overcome their challenges and achieve success.

If you need to have a developmental discussion early in the mentoring relationship, keep in mind that it could erode trust if your mentee does not believe that you truly have their best interests at heart. At this point, they won't know you well, so you'll want to emphasize your positive motives. Some great lead-ins to tough conversations include:

- "The information I'm about to share with you comes from a good place…"

- "Any advice I give you is meant to help you develop…"

- "I want to help you reach your full potential, so I will be giving you advice to help you do that. You may not like everything I have to say, however…"

- "Feedback is a gift and meant to help you develop to be your best..."

- "I have nothing but good intentions for you and want you to succeed. With that in mind, I'd like you to consider..."

Always be prepared to offer suggestions for improvement following a revelation about a development need. No one wants to be told they aren't good at something, or they aren't ready for a particular position to which they aspire. You can soften the blow and encourage your mentee by offering suggestions for ways to enhance their skills or by recommending an alternate path.

Observations Versus Insights

It's helpful to offer feedback in the form of Observations and Insights. It works like this...first, state the facts regarding what you have observed relating to your mentee's motivation, connectedness, skills, strengths, reputation, experience, etc. Then, share your insights – your interpretation of the facts. When sharing insights, you might want to include recommended actions or changes you believe would benefit your mentee.

As you offer feedback to help your mentee, you may find the need to blend Observations and Insights to help your mentee understand why and how to make changes that you believe are necessary. For example, you might make an observation about your mentee's reluctance to speak up during meetings with senior managers, and follow that with a recommendation for how to better approach the situation based on your personal experience. You can further your recommendations by offering tips, sharing resources, or making recommendations for educational opportunities.

To understand whether your mentee agrees with your Observations and Insights, ask them if your comments and recommendations resonate. Do they agree? Do they understand and appreciate your perspective, or do they have a different view? Talk about it. Listen to the points they make carefully, because you may glean additional insights into their personality and problem-solving abilities. You may hear something that will alter your thinking and/or you might have the opportunity to share your rationale. Keep in mind that it might take some time for your feedback to set in. If you feel strongly that your Observations and Insights are accurate, but your mentee is resistant, plan to revisit the discussion at a later date. Your goal should be to foster a productive and trusting relationship, not to gain dispassionate agreement from a reluctant mentee.

Finally, ask your mentee how they plan to move forward. Whether they agree with your ideas and recommendations or not, they should leave the conversation with some tangible next steps in mind. Discuss their ideas. Find out if they have questions about next steps, and offer to help. If your mentee seems stuck, take time to explore a variety of actions and activities that could help them move forward in their quest. Reassure them that although they may have a timeline in mind, life is not a race, and there is often more than one way to reach a goal.

Taking the Relationship's Temperature

Offering observations – good, bad, or neutral – can elicit unexpected responses. As you share your Observations and Insights, pay close attention to your mentee's reactions. Do they appear nervous? Surprised? Confused? Upset? Disappointed? Relieved? If they react strongly to your comments – positively or negatively – you may want to take a time out to understand why. Getting to the root of your mentee's reaction can help you understand where they're coming from, and can provide clues about how you might approach providing feedback in the future.

A mentee with low self-esteem may not instantly believe that your positive feedback is honest. Some mentees can be overwhelmed by compliments, just as they can be overwhelmed by constructive criticism. Your mentee's response could indicate the need for positive reinforcement, confidence-building exercises, and encouragement to push them out of their comfort zone.

A mentee who lacks introspection may be surprised when you reveal that they may not be ready for the role they are pursuing, and may not be receptive to a deviation from the path they planned to take. In this case, you could share specific examples to help your mentee better understand the points you're making, or share stories from your own experience to help them see value in an alternative approach. They may need some reassurance that you're not passing judgment, but offering guidance because you care and are committed to helping them grow.

Some mentees can digest a lot of feedback at once. Perhaps they've just been waiting for someone to cut to the chase and tell them the truth. Perhaps they've tried everything and are keenly aware of their own limitations. For others, too many observations in one sitting can be overwhelming. If you have a number of different points to make and you see that your mentee is becoming increasingly uncomfortable after one or two, it's probably best to save some of your thoughts for another time. As you learn more about your mentee, it will become clear what works and what does not.

It's important to note, though, that the sooner you can share your thoughts, the quicker you'll be able to develop a plan for moving forward. The longer it takes to address your observations and insights, the slower you'll move. At this point, it's your job to encourage your mentee to be transparent, keep an open mind, build skills, and approach their goals with confidence. We'll talk about getting them "unstuck" in a later chapter.

It's good practice to do a temperature check with your mentee at the start and end of every meeting, and it's always nice to end your discussions on a high note. You never want your mentee to leave a meeting feeling discouraged. Remember, you're supposed to be your mentee's greatest cheerleader, not their biggest critic.

MENTORING IN ACTION

All mentees are not eager participants – at least not initially.

According to Frank Hall, "There's a pervasive myth that says that every good mentee wants to be mentored. Even more pervasive is the belief that the best mentees are the ones who approach the mentor first."

When asked about his "best" mentoring experience, Frank paused, and then said, "Every relationship – well, almost every relationship – has merit. I've been fortunate to have some mentees who have gone on to do great things and to become great leaders. But honestly, one of my most rewarding mentorships was with an unassuming guy named Jim.

Jim is an interesting character. When I became the Vice President of Sales, I inherited a team. Jim was one of my reps; at the time, he was two levels below me. One day, I flew out to ride with him and to visit some customers. He picked me up at the airport looking like he had just rolled out of bed. We stopped for breakfast. The plan was to review our schedule and discuss the day's meetings. As we pulled into the parking lot, Jim opened the car door while the car was still running, and a bunch of papers flew out; a few slid beneath the car.

I grabbed the door handle and planned to jump out – as any man would who was riding with a disheveled rep who opens his car door before making a complete stop. In the calmest voice possible, I said, "Jim, I think you dropped something."

Jim leaned his head out, and looked under the car. Then, to my surprise, he proceeded to back the car up, stop, get out, retrieve his account plans, and pull back into the parking space. He shoved the crumpled paperwork into his briefcase – obviously unaffected by the event – smiled, and said, 'Okay, let's go in.'"

What happened next? Well, Frank listened intently as Jim reviewed his tire-marked plans. Then, the two headed out to see some customers. Frank worried that the disaster would continue. He said, "I honestly did not have high hopes for the day. In fact, I was wondering how the guy got hired, and was questioning the judgment of the District Manager who had put him in charge of some of the company's largest accounts. But the guy blew me away! He was, without a doubt, one of the smartest, most competent reps I'd ever met. He knew our products inside and out, yes, but more than that, he understood the customer's business. It was obvious that our customers relied on him as a trusted resource to help them with their transportation needs, but they also turned to him for advice on packaging and labeling – neither of which were services we offered.

Along our two-day journey in the field, I learned quite a bit about Jim. I learned that he had an engineering background, that he started with the company when he was in college, and that his promotion into sales was prompted by a long-term customer who threatened to leave unless Jim was assigned to manage their account. He had been their service manager for years, and they had burned through many less-knowledgeable reps. So, the District Manager at the time gave him the job. And, as they say, the rest is history. But I also learned that Jim really wanted to move into management and that, although he had interviewed several times for various leadership positions, he had been disappointed time and time again. Jim told me that he couldn't believe he was being passed up for promotions when he had led the company in sales for 5 years running. He truly had no idea what could be holding him back, but I knew."

Frank went on to say, "As impressed as I was with Jim's capability, I realized that despite his incredible talent, he was going to sit on the bench for the rest of his career, if he couldn't do something about his image and change people's perceptions of him as a potential leader."

After working together for two full days, the pair met to discuss the experience. Frank put his hand on Jim's shoulder and said, "Jim, you're one of the smartest guys I've come across in this business, and I think you have a ton of potential to move up in the company *if* you are willing to make some changes." Jim was caught off guard, at first, but he respected Frank, so he listened. At the end of the conversation, Frank offered to mentor Jim, and Jim graciously agreed. For the next two years, Frank met with Jim in person or virtually once a month.

Today, Jim is a successful District Manager and Frank continues to mentor him.

DISCOVERY TOOL

Use this tool to think about the conversation you plan to have with your mentee, and record your thoughts following the meeting.

Part 1: Observations and Insights from Prior Meetings
Observations from prior meetings:

_____

_____

_____

_____

_____

Insights from prior meetings:

_____

_____

_____

_____

I plan to recommend:

_____

_____

_____

_____

I want my mentee to know that I am offering Observations and Insights with the best of intentions. So, I plan to lead into the conversation by:

_____

_____

_____

_____

_____

Part 2: Next Steps

Observations related to my mentee's response to my feedback include:

_____

_____

_____

_____

_____

Insights I gained from my mentee's reaction include:

_____

_____

_____

_____

_____

Based on these insights, I plan to consider the following when providing feedback in the future:

_____

_____

_____

_____

_____

_____

_____

Topics to discuss during the next meeting:

_____

_____

_____

_____

_____

_____

_____

_____

_____

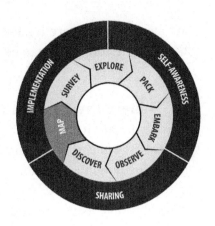

Chapter 6

MAP: GOAL-SETTING

*"Successful people turn everyone who can help them
into sometime mentors!"*
—John Crosby

Mentoring relationships are shaped by the stated goals your mentee is pursuing. Many mentees set out to find a mentor with specific objectives in mind. For example, a mentee may want to know how to best position themselves for a coveted promotion, or they may be interested in ways to increase their visibility in the industry. They may want to expand their network, or they may seek advice regarding the best next steps in their journey. As a mentor, you'll want to do whatever you can to help.

By the time you reach the "Map" stage, you will have had a series of meetings with your mentee. You should have a good idea about where they want to go in their professional life and what they hope to accomplish. You should be familiar with their background and experience, and should have an opinion about whether they have the knowledge and skills to get to achieve their aims.

Your mentee may intend to reach their destination in ten years, five years, two years, or six months. When thinking about mentoring, it's important to define goals that can be accomplished within a designated period of time, specifically through the duration of the mentorship. If your mentee's goals are longer-term, you should work with them to establish milestones that can be accomplished in the near-term.

Ask, "Where Are You Headed?"

Applying a critical eye to your mentee's goals at this point in the relationship will certainly benefit the partnership moving forward. By establishing tangible, unambiguous targets for mentoring, you'll set an end point that, if achieved, will move your mentee closer to achieving their ambitions. You can start by ensuring that your mentee's goals are well-defined, realistic, and aligned with their career aspirations. Revisit the goals they shared during your initial meeting. Have they evolved through discussion? Do both of you agree that the goals are reasonable and attainable during your time together?

To determine whether your mentee is starting with the "right" goals, you might want to begin with the big picture. Challenge your mentee to describe where they want to be in three, five, or ten years. Ask them to describe where they will be at the pinnacle of their career. Then, work backwards from there. If you start with the small tasks, you might inadvertently guide your mentee to an unanticipated result. To explore your mentee's long-term vision, ask questions like:

- What is your ultimate career goal?

- What role will you have when you retire?

- Are you working toward specific career accomplishments?

- Who is your career role model right now?

- If everything works out the way you hope, what will you be doing ten years from now?

- What would you do if you knew you couldn't fail?

- If you didn't need to work for a living, how would you spend your time?

Your mentee may say they want to be the CEO of a Fortune 500 company, or close $10 million in business for their employer. They may want to quit their job and start their own business, or leave the private sector to pursue a career in politics. When you're clear about the desired destination, you'll be in a good position to help map out a route.

Before you get too excited, you might want to do a reality check. Just because your mentee *wants* to be CEO, doesn't mean they're positioned to be one, or that they have time to develop the skills they need to rise to that position. Likewise, if a salesperson wants to close $10 million in sales, but has never had a year over $300 thousand, their goal may be unrealistic, at least within the lifetime of your mentorship. Is it possible for a person to jump from a manager to CEO? Maybe. Could a salesperson come across a huge opportunity that could magnify their sales exponentially? Possibly. But both are certainly a long shot. As a mentor, it's up to you to be a voice of reason without diminishing your mentee's drive or ambition.

Alternatively, you could have a mentee whose goals aren't ambitious enough. Your mentee might not realize that they have the capacity to achieve more. If you suspect that your mentee's goals may be inhibited in some way, try to uncover the "why" behind their limitations. Does your mentee have blind spots and unrecognized talent? Do they suffer from poor self-esteem? Have they been told that they couldn't do X, Y or Z because they lack a college degree? Often, limitations can be self-imposed. If you think your mentee can and should do more, let them know. With encouragement, you might prompt your mentee to set their sights a bit higher.

Redirecting Aspirations

Of course, trying to reorient your mentee's goals may be more difficult than it sounds. Redirecting a mentee who is set on a plan can be like changing the course of a battleship. It could require a lot of effort, and be a slow and tedious process. You want to challenge your mentee to become their best self, but you don't want to push your mentee too far too quickly and risk damaging the relationship. On the other hand, if a mentee has been committed to a goal for some time, it might be tough to convince them that it isn't worth pursuing. While you may recognize right away that realizing their dream may require more than a stretch, consider keeping that belief to yourself (at least temporarily) while you work to adjust your mentee's expectations and goals.

The typical mentorship lasts about twelve months. But twelve months can pass quickly. If your mentee comes up with ten things they'd like to accomplish during your work together, you'll need to help them focus and prioritize. Help your mentee pare back to no more than three goals that support their longer-term objectives. Three significant goals are more than enough to tackle during a 12 month mentorship.

A Real-Life Example

Jennifer, a highly motivated 28-year-old salesperson for a global technology company, set a goal to become a Vice President before the age of 40. She did her due diligence and mapped out a plan to accomplish her goal months before she met her mentor. She knew that to become a VP, she would need experience in key functional areas of the business. She determined that she would need to secure a management position within the next nine months. From there, she would seek positions with escalating responsibility, remaining in each position for no more than two years. Informed with an org chart, Jennifer identified the job titles that would lead her to success, and contacted Human Resources to obtain the requirements for each position. She shared her well-considered plan with her mentor, Brian, at their first meeting.

Brian was impressed with the amount of effort Jennifer had put into the plan, and thought that her objectives were ambitious, but doable. However, before establishing goals for their mentorship, he thought it was important to better understand Jennifer's motivations. Through the conversation, Brian learned that his mentee wanted to become a Vice President because she wanted to inspire and lead people. In fact, Jennifer was already a resource to sales colleagues who often turned to her for advice. She enjoyed helping others, and appreciated the benefits of collaborating with others, as she did when participating on a team chartered to improve employee engagement.

Mentor: "Your plan seems to be well thought out. So, what's your next step?

Mentee: "Well, I saw a posting for an IT Consultant. I've learned a lot about uncovering client needs by selling our solutions. So, I think I'll go for it!"

Mentor: "That's interesting. An IT Consultant? Can you tell me more about the position?"

The mentee handed her mentor the job description. He read it, and asked some questions.

Mentor: "Why is the role interesting to you?"

Mentee: "Well, to start with, it's a Level 7. So, it's the equivalent of a first-line manager role on the sales side. It's two grades above my current role, but I think sales gives me a unique perspective, and I've had exceptional reviews. I honestly think I have a good chance."

Mentor: "Can I ask a question?

Mentee: "Sure."

Mentor: "Do you have a description of the VP role that you hope to obtain in the future?"

Mentee: "Funny you should ask. I actually tried to find one, but you know, they don't post those jobs very often." (The mentee laughed.)

Mentor: "If you were to guess, what knowledge, skills and experience do you think someone needs to be an effective Vice President at this organization?"

Mentee: "I guess that depends on which VP role we're talking about."

Mentor: "How many VPs are there?"

Mentee: "Four. We have a VP of Sales and Marketing, VP of Operations, VP of Consulting Services, and a VP of HR."

Mentor: "Which role interests you, Vice President of Consulting Services?"

Mentee: "Hmmmm. I'm not sure…maybe VP of Sales and Marketing."

Mentor: "Okay, then let's take a step back. What position do you think you'll be in just prior to moving into a VP role?"

Mentee: "Well, you have to be a Director before becoming a VP, so I'll probably be a Director of Something."

Mentor: "What do you know about that role?"

Mentee: "Well, I do have a posting for a Director's position that happens to be open now. It talks about an innovative leader, someone with dynamic presence, who can work well with teams across the Organization."

Mentor: "Does that sound like something you'd be interested in in the future?"

Mentee: "Definitely! It sounds like my dream job."

Mentor: "Is there anything in that description that doesn't appeal to you?"

Mentee: "Not that I can see."

Mentor: "Now, let's take a look at the posting for the IT Consultant. How do they describe that position?"

Mentee: "Works independently, writes reports and documentation, requires exceptional technical skills, may travel extensively."

Mentor: "Does that sound like something you're interested in?"

Mentee: "To be honest, not really. But I know I could do it. It's two levels above my current position, and I would only do the job for two years…max. I think I could do anything for two years! And I'd get to know more about that part of the business."

Mentor: "Other than the fact that the pay grade for the role is equivalent to that of a first-line manager, how does the role of IT Consultant fit within your larger career aspirations?'

Mentee: "I guess it doesn't really, but there aren't any openings for first-line managers, and I don't want to wait too long. They don't really like to move people out of sales mid-year, so I need to act while I can."

Mentor: "Well, all of that makes sense, but maybe there's another path that will better align with your ten-year plan *and* will involve options that you will actually enjoy along the way."

Mentee: "I guess I see your point."

Through supportive dialogue and discussion, Brian encouraged Jennifer to pause and think about her strategy in the context of her ultimate career aspirations. The pair worked together to identify options and set goals that would better serve the mentee. Jennifer's new list of options included:

- Finding a special project that would allow her to increase her exposure without moving away from the sales role in which she was so successful

- Working with Brian to strengthen her network by building more contacts in leadership positions

- Networking to learn about possible postings for first-line managers

- Considering a position in Marketing (even if it's a lateral move) that would allow her to expand her functional knowledge while making best use of her skills and abilities

Jennifer chose to look for a position in Marketing. With that goal in mind, the pair was able to define next steps and milestones to launch the mentorship:

- Jennifer was approached to participate on a cross-functional team responsible for launching the Company's next new product. Initially, she considered declining the offer so she could focus on obtaining the IT Consultant position, but with that no longer on the table, she was able to say "yes" to the invitation. (week one)

- Brian learned that Jennifer had contacts in the Department, so it was logical to ask if they would meet with her to offer their perspectives on potential roles. Jennifer agreed to schedule time with each of them. (within two weeks)

- Next, the pair assessed Jennifer's skills and abilities with a Marketing role in mind. They agreed that it would be worth her time to invest in improving her presentation skills, so Jennifer decided to sign up for a public speaking course. (during Month 1)

- The New Product Launch Team had already scheduled their first meeting. The Marketing Director was expected to attend. Brian suggested that Jennifer find time to introduce herself in an effort to expand her network. (during Month 2)

- After connecting with the Marketing Director, Jennifer and Brian would discuss ways to further the relationship (i.e., ask to meet for a cup of coffee, sign up for the Communications subcommittee formed to advance the new product launch, and/ or ask to shadow someone in the Department for a day). (during Month 3)

This is just what you'd hope to see from a mentee and mentor in terms of potential next steps. But this couldn't have happened if the mentor hadn't first kindly, but firmly, guided his mentee toward a more aligned goal. By considering the mentee's aspirations, coupled with the limitations of a 12-month mentoring time frame, the mentor was able to work with the mentee to define actions and activities that would enable her to advance her goals while enjoying the journey. If you recognize that your mentee's goals are too lofty, too short-term, too vague or too easily achieved, step in to help rewrite them.

Setting SMART Goals

Whether you determine that your mentee needs to completely overhaul their goals or you think they simply need to be tweaked, it's important to ensure that their goals are actionable. Writer and philosopher Elbert Hubbard said this:

> "Many people fail in life, not for lack of ability or brains or even courage but simply because they have never organized their energies around a goal."

And...

> "Know what you want to do, hold the thought firmly, and do every day what should be done, and every sunset will see you that much nearer to your goal."

Although there is some debate as to who should receive credit for first use of the acronym, S.M.A.R.T., there is little argument that S.M.A.R.T. is the most commonly used tool for quality goal-setting. There is a slight deviation in how S.M.A.R.T. is defined from author to author, but for our purposes we will say that a goal should be: Specific, Measureable, Attainable, Realistic, and Timely. A goal built with this in mind should be clear and quantifiable.

Here are some tips for setting goals that are **SMART**:

Specific. It is important to ensure that every goal is well-defined. A vague goal, such as "Set more appointments with prospects," is useless. How will you know if your mentee has been successful at reaching their goal if you don't establish what they mean by "more"? And if you don't have a set target, how can you expect your mentee to, "Set *more* appointments?" Specificity is critical.

Likewise, if you ask your mentee to list their goals and they say, "One of my goals is to improve my presentation skills," we'd argue that their goal should be more precise. A better, more definitive goal would be to: "Join Toastmasters and attend at least two meetings a month to improve my presentation skills."

Some people benefit from visualization. By creating a picture in their minds, they are able to envision how they might achieve their goals. If you think your mentee might appreciate the power of a mental image, suggest that they use the Five W's to further define their goals. Encourage them to answer the following questions:

- <u>Wh</u>at do I want to achieve?

- <u>Wh</u>y does this goal make sense?

- <u>Wh</u>ose participation will be needed to accomplish the goal?

- <u>Wh</u>ere will I accomplish my work?

- <u>Wh</u>en will I achieve my goal?

When the Five W's are applied to the example we just discussed, it might look something like this:

Goal: Join Toastmasters and attend at least two meetings a month to improve my presentation skills.

- "After doing some research, I found that The Downtown Toastmasters are the best group for me. I have contacted the club president who invited me to their next meeting." (<u>Wh</u>ose participation will be needed to accomplish the goal?)

- "I want to join the Toastmasters to become a better presenter and improve the quality and impact of my presentations." (<u>Wh</u>at do I want to achieve?)

- "Club meetings are once-a-month for 1-2 hours. I will also need to reserve time to complete my assignments." (<u>Wh</u>ere their work will occur?)

- "Learning is project-based. Project 1 should take approximately three months to complete. If I start in January, I should have completed the course by the end of March. (During what time-frame? (<u>When</u>))

- "Participating in this club will help me because I will need strong presentation skills if I plan to become an effective leader." (<u>Why</u> does this goal makes sense?)

Measurable. In addition to being specific, a SMART goal should also be quantifiable. That means that there should be an identified yardstick for every objective. Without an agreed-to measurement, it will be difficult for you and your mentee to evaluate their progress.

Let's say that your mentee sets a goal to: "Expand my network." As stated, the goal doesn't say how big they want their network to be or who should be in it. Restating the goal with specific dimensions will ensure that their progress can be measured. A better goal would be to: "Expand my network to include a leader from every department and at least three members of the Senior Leadership Team."

Measures not related to time may include one or more of the following factors:

- Percentage improvement (10% above the prior year)

- Numerical goal (dollars, performance rank, salary increase, etc.)

- Frequency (two times per month, once a quarter, etc.)

- Quantity (six direct reports, four new contracts, etc.)

- Quality (Highly Proficient rating)

If your mentee's goals are specific and measurable, you'll be in a good position to monitor and support their progress.

Attainable. By nature, SMART goals must also be within reach. Your mentee must believe that it is truly possible to achieve their goal, and they must be able to see a path to accomplishment. To determine whether your mentee believes that the goal they've set is realistic, ask probing questions about how they're going to get from where they are now to where they want to be. Can they describe the required steps or do they struggle to articulate the tasks and activities that need to be accomplished? If a goal is just a wish or dream, it's not currently attainable. But if you can get your mentee to work through the steps required to achieve success, it may become possible.

Realistic. A goal may be attainable, while at the same time unrealistic. To be realistic, your mentee must be willing to invest the appropriate amount of effort required to accomplish their objective. We all know that it is possible, for instance, to run a mile in less than four minutes, but not everyone is driven to accomplish this goal. If your mentee believes they can achieve a goal, *and* they are willing to do what it takes to attain it, then we'd say that the goal is realistic.

If, for example, your mentee's goal is to earn a Ph.D. in management in the next 3 years, it may be realistic if they have already earned a bachelor's degree, and are willing to invest the time and effort to attend that is required to qualify for the distinction. However, if they don't have a degree, bachelor's or masters, and/or they don't have the time to attend the required classes, their goal may not be realistic. That doesn't mean that their goal cannot be accomplished in the future. For now, you can help your mentee by either redefining or restating their goal, or by helping them choose a different goal altogether.

Timely. Another critical aspect of SMART goals is that they are set to be accomplished within a defined period of time. An achievement date provides a means of determining whether a goal has been met. For example, if your mentee sets out to complete five sales presentations by June 1st, but completes only three by that date, it will be easy to see that their goal has yet to be achieved.

Setting a timely goal puts boundaries around the target activity or achievement, and helps to create a sense of urgency. Without a deadline, a goal is just a wish. Someday it may be completed, but if it's not time-bound, it will be hard to gauge whether the goal has been successfully met.

Of course, just because your mentee sets a certain goal at the start of your mentorship doesn't mean it won't change mid-stream. Your mentee might be influenced by others they encounter during your mentorship or by a book you recommend. Insights and advice may challenge the mentee to revise or refine their goal. This is perfectly fine. Your mentee should keep you informed about the goals that they are working toward, but modifications can indicate that your mentee is becoming more in tune with what is right for them. So, offer support as they strive for clarity.

Getting a Second Opinion

As you assist your mentee in setting goals that are specific, measurable, attainable, realistic and timely, you may find that you could use some additional insight into your mentee's strengths, weaknesses, personality and reputation in order to better advise them. A 360-degree evaluation, or similar comprehensive approach to collecting insights, can be a useful tool.

The practice of 360-degree feedback involves gathering input from the individuals closely surrounding your mentee. This may include your mentee's supervisor, four to eight colleagues, direct reports and customers. Depending on your mentee's job, you could also ask for feedback from suppliers and other support staff with whom they regularly interact. The idea is to gather perceptions about your mentee's performance from those who work around them. To complete the circle, you should also ask the mentee to complete a self-assessment. The findings from these evaluations can be used to help your mentee understand their own strengths and weaknesses and to identify potential professional developmental opportunities.

If you can initiate a 360-degree evaluation, or review the results from a recent evaluation of the mentee, you'll likely learn more about their capabilities and gain insights into how they are perceived. This understanding can help you offer appropriate guidance and recommendations. Through the evaluations, you may discover that your mentee has a high personal opinion that is not shared by those around them. Or, conversely, you may find that your mentee is humble to a fault and is not highlighting qualities or accomplishments that are obvious to others.

As a mentor it's your job to gather information, process it, discern the "truth," and use it to offer guidance that can help your mentee set SMART-er goals.

GOAL SETTING

Use this tool to help your mentee evaluate and further refine their goals.

Part 1: Mentees with Goals

Some mentees may have well-constructed goals as you enter into the mentorship, while others may struggle to determine where they want to go. Ask your mentee to share their goals. Capture them, in your mentee's own words, in the space provided below:

Goal #1:

_____

_____

_____

_____

Goal #2:

_____

_____

_____

_____

Goal #3:

_____

_____

_____

_____

Observations:

_____

_____

_____

_____

_____

Insights:

_____

_____

_____

_____

_____

Recommendations:

_____

_____

_____

_____

_____

Part 2: Making Goals Smart-er

Help your mentee ensure that their goals are actionable by making them S.M.A.R.T. Select a goal from Part 1 and apply the model using the S.M.A.R.T. Chart. (See the example below.)

Goal (Example):
To improve my presentation skills within the next six months.

S.M.A.R.T. Chart			
S.M.A.R.T. Component	**Evidence**	**✓**	**Recommendation**
Specific	To improve my presentation skills		Make it more specific by stating "how" you plan to improve your skills. Add the types of skills for even greater clarity.
Measurable			Receive an "Exceptional" rating on my next Business Review presentation.
Attainable			Determine what it will take to make this goal attainable.
Realistic			Establish a plan including the steps required to achieve the goal.
Timely	within the next six months		

Further clarify the goal by adding:

- ❑ <u>W</u>hat do I want to achieve? *Achieve an "Exceptional" rating*
- ❑ <u>W</u>hy does this goal make sense? *I will demonstrate that I am capable of being a leader*
- ❑ <u>W</u>hose participation will be needed to accomplish the goal? *My mentor*
- ❑ <u>W</u>here will I accomplish my work? *Complete the online course; practice with my mentor*
- ❑ <u>W</u>hen will I achieve my goal? *Within the next six months*

Revised goal:

To improve my presentation skills within the next six months by completing the Mastering PowerPoint course and achieving an "Exceptional" rating on my next Business Review presentation.

Use the space below to evaluate your mentee's goals.

Goal #1:

_____

_____

_____

S.M.A.R.T. Chart			
S.M.A.R.T. Component	Evidence	✓	Recommendation
Specific			
Measurable			
Attainable			
Realistic			
Timely			

Further clarify the goal by adding:

- ☐ What do I want to achieve?
- ☐ Why does this goal make sense?
- ☐ Whose participation will be needed to accomplish the goal?
- ☐ Where will I accomplish my work?
- ☐ When will I achieve my goal?

Revised goal:

_____

_____

_____

_____

Goal #2:

_____

_____

_____

S.M.A.R.T. Chart			
S.M.A.R.T. Component	Evidence	✓	Recommendation
Specific			
Measurable			
Attainable			
Realistic			
Timely			

Further clarify the goal by adding:

☐ What do I want to achieve?
☐ Why does this goal make sense?
☐ Whose participation will be needed to accomplish the goal?
☐ Where will I accomplish my work?
☐ When will I achieve my goal?

Revised goal:

_____

_____

_____

_____

Goal #3:

_____

_____

_____

S.M.A.R.T. Chart			
S.M.A.R.T. Component	**Evidence**	✓	**Recommendation**
Specific			
Measurable			
Attainable			
Realistic			
Timely			

Further clarify the goal by adding:

- ❑ What do I want to achieve?
- ❑ Why does this goal make sense?
- ❑ Whose participation will be needed to accomplish the goal?
- ❑ Where will I accomplish my work?
- ❑ When will I achieve my goal?

Revised goal:

_____

_____

_____

_____

Topics to discuss during the next meeting:

_____

_____

_____

_____

_____

_____

_____

_____

_____

_____

_____

_____

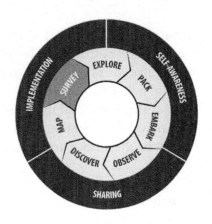

Chapter 7

SURVEY: PLAN NEXT STEPS

*"Mentoring is a brain to pick, an ear to listen, and
a push in the right direction."*
—*John Crosby*

As you close the loop on the feedback and recommendations you've provided your mentee, it's time to revisit their goals and plan for what happens next. Your role as mentor is to nudge your mentee in the right direction, give them encouragement when they need it, and help them learn from each and every experience. But you're not their teacher, their parent or their drill sergeant. You can't, and shouldn't try, to force them to do what you think is best, even if you have the best of intentions.

You can drive the goal-setting process, but don't try to drive specific goals. You can share your Observations and Insights as to whether your mentee has set the "right" goals, and you can give feedback regarding whether the goals are realistic, attainable or even worth pursuing. But ultimately, your mentee has to choose where to invest their time and attention, and to determine which goals resonate.

You can help by providing a perspective that your mentee may not have. They may not recognize their own strengths, strengths which you can spot from a mile away. Consequently, they may not be reaching high enough or stretching far enough outside their comfort zone to arrive at their full potential. Conversely, your mentee may not recognize the weaknesses that are sabotaging their efforts to accomplish a particular goal. By pointing out situations that support your observations, you can help your mentee develop strategies to overcome or minimize their weaknesses or adjust their goals to account for them. You can be the catalyst that prompts your mentee to evaluate their goals, but you cannot be the author and expect your mentee to be successful.

Confirm Comprehension

At this point, it's important to confirm that you and your mentee are on the same page. Do you understand each other? Are you communicating well? Is there a level of trust that allows you to share Observations and Insights that can help your mentee progress? Does your mentee welcome feedback, even if it's unflattering? If your mentee is to progress you will need to ensure that the two of you are in sync, and that you and your mentee believe that the mentorship can be successful.

While you may believe that you have been crystal clear when sharing information about your mentee's skills, abilities, and behavior, your mentee may not have heard everything you had to say. Now it's time to confirm that your feedback resonates. Offering challenging Observations and Insights could create resistance that might not surface immediately. Look to your mentee's responses over time to help you determine whether they agree with your feedback and are ready to change their behavior accordingly.

Perhaps you observed that your mentee often takes credit for the work of others on their team, and you shared your insights. Was your mentee responsive to the feedback? If not, what else can you do to help them recognize their blind spot and address this issue that, if unresolved, could be a detriment to your mentee in the future?

Does your mentee "get" that pursuing a master's degree won't guarantee a promotion, even though it's been their goal for many years? When some people receive information that is contrary to their own plans, they shut down or zone out. If you think your feedback isn't getting through to your mentee, you need to find a way to break through to make sure that your mentee is truly listening. If you believe the feedback is worth sharing, then it should be important enough to elicit a response. Your mentee's career success could depend on it.

Once you've succeeded in getting your mentee to listen to what you have to say, it's important to confirm that they now know how to translate your feedback and move forward with your recommendations. It's one thing to tell your mentee that their hip-length hair makes some leaders uncomfortable, but it's quite another to discuss and agree on what they will do to improve the situation. Discussing the "why" could prove to be the impetus for change.

The "What and Why" technique can be a useful tool for gaining buy in. Be specific when telling your mentee "What" you observed. You might say, "This is our fifth meeting. I've noticed that every time we get together, you seem rushed and a bit disorganized." Then, share the "Why": "I didn't comment earlier, because I thought you were just nervous, but now I feel the need to say something, because I think it could be affecting people's perceptions of you." You might have to repeat the same observation more than once with more than one example to be sure your mentee understands that your Observations and Insights are important, and that you wouldn't suggest a change if you didn't think it would make a difference. When offering feedback for a second time on the same issue, you might say, "When we met in your office, I noticed that you seemed a bit preoccupied. It seemed like you had a lot on your plate that day. I understand why you might not want to say "no" when presented with an opportunity, but sometimes that's the most important thing you can do. By saying "no", you'll have less on your plate, and more time to focus on your priorities. At this point in your career, it's important to show people that you can make the tough decisions, even if it means turning down some opportunities." By providing tough feedback and being brutally honest –even when you'd prefer not to be – you'll solidify your role as a trusted advisor who has your mentee's best interests at heart. Most of all, you'll help your mentee evolve and grow.

To confirm that your mentee has heard you, ask them to repeat what you said and suggest that they translate your feedback into their own words. Then, ask them to suggest next steps before offering your own recommendations. Capture your mentee's agreements to reference later, and offer to help. Keeping notes in your journal will help you recall your mentee's commitments, and remind you of what you discussed and why it was important to your mentee's progress.

Sticking to Deadlines

Timelines will also be important in assessing your mentee's progress. How well is your mentee tracking to their goals? Have they hit the expected milestones? Are they moving more quickly or more slowly than you both expected? Why? Has your mentee achieved any of their goals within the target time frame? If not, why not? How has the mentee's progress, or lack of progress, impacted their ability to reach their stated goal? Should the timeline be revised or extended? At what point will the goal be expunged if it can't be met? (There is likely a drop-dead date after which the goal ceases to be worth pursuing.)

If progress has been slower than anticipated, perhaps you and your mentee haven't broken the goal down into reasonable tasks. It's human nature to get stuck on a problem when you don't know what to do next. If your mentee has stalled in pursuit of their goals, they may lack a clear path to achieving them. Use your experience to counsel your mentee on what is reasonable to expect within a given time frame, such as a week or a month. They may not realize that the goal they thought should take two weeks is more likely to take two months, or vice versa. That's where your skills and background can make a big difference. With reasonable expectations, and goals broken down into chunks, your mentee may be able to move forward more quickly.

If your mentee has trouble breaking down their goals, you can help them by understanding their ultimate objective and deadline, and working backwards to figure out what needs to be done by when in order to accomplish their goal(s). Let's say your mentee wants to complete a specific certification within the next six months; look ahead six months and choose a target date for goal completion. Then, set monthly and weekly objectives that will ultimately lead to the achievement of the greater goal.

Collapsing some larger goals into manageable accomplishments may require you and your mentee to learn more about the tasks and activities associated with achieving the goals. For instance, if your mentee hopes to publish an article in an industry trade magazine, they might benefit from reviewing the magazine's submission requirements. If they want to learn how to effectively manage complex projects, they might meet with someone who is known for their exceptional project management skills. Until you know what is required to achieve a goal, it will be difficult to create a path comprised of discrete tasks and activities. If you and your mentee are unclear about the requirements for reaching the goal, challenge your mentee to do some research before your next meeting. If you are going to make progress, they will need to gather enough information to be able to confidently set tasks, objectives, and deadlines.

Are You the Best Mentor You Can Be?

In addition to reviewing goals and setting new ones for your mentee, take the opportunity to ask for feedback from your mentee regarding how effectively you're meeting their needs. Keep in mind that your mentee might be reluctant to speak frankly about your shortcomings for fear of upsetting you. With enough encouragement and reassurance, they should become more confident in offering their own observations. In time, you may be able to elicit insights and suggestions that will help you improve and become an even better mentor.

Some ways to lead off your request for feedback might include:

- "I value our working relationship and want to be sure you're receiving all that you need to be successful. What are a couple of ways I can be of better service to you?"

- "You've made great strides in the last few months and I want to be sure you continue to progress. What else can I do, or do differently, to make that possible?"

- "I'm sure you came into this mentorship with some expectations for how I could help you. Am I providing all the support and guidance you hoped for? If not, how else can I help?"

- "Since a mentorship is a two-way street, I was hoping you could help me do a better job of helping you. What do I do that you find most helpful? How could I improve? Please, don't hold back."

Tell your mentee that you will make it a routine practice to ask for their feedback. Ask them to note your strengths and weaknesses, just as you are monitoring theirs. Knowing that you'll be posing the question again may help your mentee to be prepared to share Observations and Insights at your next planning meeting.

As you wrap up your meeting, take time to congratulate your mentee on the progress they've made so far. Every mentor and mentee relationship will progress at a different rate. You may reach this point midway through the duration of the mentorship, or not until you come to the end of the agreed upon timeline.

MENTORING IN ACTION

When asked about the benefits of mentoring, corporate accountant Wendy Reed said, "It's been great to watch my mentee blossom and become who she was truly meant to be. The most rewarding part has been surfacing the strengths and capabilities she hadn't been accessing or valuing. I love witnessing her new found self-confidence, even in high-stakes situations that would have intimidated her in the past. But honestly, I'd say I've learned as much through mentoring as she has."

Wendy asked for input from her mentee at the end of each meeting. "Early on, I think my mentee was hesitant to share her opinions – in part because she was new to mentoring and didn't know what to expect, and in part because she didn't want to hurt my feelings. In time, she grew more comfortable being honest and open, and that was really helpful."

But Wendy felt that their formal debrief at the end of the mentorship offered the most significant insights. "Toward the end of our mentorship, we met to talk about what worked well and where I could improve when mentoring future mentees. I am eternally grateful for my mentee's insights and candid feedback." With the entire experience behind them, Wendy's mentee was able to reflect on their time together and share her thoughts. From that experience, Wendy learned:

- It's best to wait until trust is high before confronting potentially difficult topics.
- Being overly positive can be perceived as insincere.
- Appropriately challenging your mentee can reveal potential blind spots and can positively alter their career choices and paths.
- Mentoring someone is an important responsibility that requires time and commitment from both parties.

Wendy has recently engaged in mentorships with two new mentees. She is carrying her lessons forward and is continuing to seek feedback to further improve her mentoring skills. She has come to realize that each mentoring relationship is unique and should be treated as such. "Every mentoring relationship is a new experience. Mentoring gives you the opportunity to have an impact on others, while at the same time giving you the chance to learn more about yourself," says Wendy.

MENTORSHIP SURVEY

Use this tool to reflect on the time you've spent with your mentee to date and to plan next steps.

Number of meetings so far: _____

Time remaining in the mentorship: _____

Part 1: Strength of the Mentoring Relationship
Themes/trends observed over time:

_____

_____

_____

_____

Use the space below to evaluate the mentoring relationship
at the current time based on the Success Factors.

Success Factor	Evaluation				
	Low				High
	1	2	3	4	5
Trust					
Receptivity to Feedback					
Willingness to Change					
Progress Toward Goals					
Other:					
Other:					

Feedback from my mentee:

_____

_____

_____

_____

I can improve my mentoring efforts by:

_____

_____

_____

_____

Part 2: Next Steps
Our mentorship:

☐ Is coming to a close   ☐ Will continue   ☐ Has an unclear
    and will end on   through __/__/__   future
    __/__/__

Topics to discuss during the next meeting:

_____

_____

_____

_____

I plan to recommend:

_____

_____

_____

_____

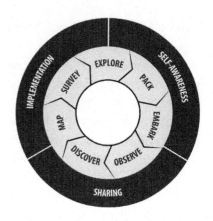

Chapter 8

MENTORING TRANSITIONS

"Look on every exit as being an entrance somewhere else."
—Tom Stoppard

The Mentoring Cycle

So, you've worked your way around the Mentoring Journey, moving through the stages from Explore to Pack to Embark to Observe to Discover to Map and finally to Survey. You've guided your mentee through Self-Awareness, Implementation and Follow-Up. By this point you have, without a doubt, learned a lot about your mentee, and if you are lucky, you learned something about yourself.

In mentoring, progress is the measure of success. Whether your mentee has met their ultimate goals or simply reached important milestones along the way, the triumph is in the journey. Perhaps your mentee is even more driven toward their initial aspiration and is better positioned for victory as a result of meeting you. Or perhaps they realized that the path they were on was never really the one that was meant for them. Either way, the mentee is likely changed by the experience.

Your mentee may have reached their pinnacle or they may have hit a plateau on their trek. Regardless, the end of any cycle is not the time to stop growing, in fact, it's the time to take a quantum leap toward your destiny. Keep that in mind as you approach the chasm between

Survey and Explore; you should reflect on your progress, but move forward and set new goals.

Some mentor/mentee relationships continue through a lifetime, while others may last only a few months. But rest assured it's not the duration of the relationship that's important, it's the quality of the interactions. Mentoring relationships generally follow a circular pattern, beginning with discussions about dreams and aspirations, progressing over time as goals are realized, and culminating with new intentions and targets. What began with an initial get-to-know-you meeting should by now have evolved into a kinship of sorts – different from a friendship, more than a coach, but definitely a trusted advisor. In all likelihood, you and your mentee have become accustomed to your differing personalities, communication styles, and views on life. Even if you are very different people, you have probably come to understand and respect each other.

You have likely established a rhythm (meeting weekly, bimonthly or monthly). You have probably landed on a preferred method for communicating (in person, via phone, via skype or email). You may converse regularly or sporadically. Your mentorship has probably developed its own unique personality, one that works for both of you. It may not look like past mentoring relationships or be well-suited to partnerships that lie ahead. That's the beauty of mentoring, every pairing takes on a life of its own. Every adventure is different and every expedition moves at a different pace.

You may have discovered, for example, that impromptu meetings are useful between more formal monthly sit-down review sessions. You and your mentee might have found a benefit to occasionally working together for several hours to prepare for high-stakes presentations. Or you might have found that your mentee appreciates the ability to simply reach out with a text when they need you. A quick question and a prompt response may be all that they need to stay on track.

Unexpected situations can come up that call for timely review and discussion. Your willingness and ability to carve out extra time when needed can go a long way toward supporting your mentee and developing a trusting relationship. On the other hand, too-frequent contact could be disruptive. Setting boundaries will protect your time and will teach your mentee about the value of planning, discernment, and respect for others. A frank discussion about your availability, and some agreements around expectations and process, can go a long way toward establishing norms that meet your needs and allow you to respond to theirs.

Moving On

As you reach the end of the Survey stage, you may be approaching the end of a formal mentoring program, or simply transitioning to a new goal. Either way, it's important to take time to close the books on your current journey and determine where you'll go next. For many pairings, the end of a formal program or agreed to time frame could be the end of routine communications, as well as the end of the mentorship as you have known it. So, you may want to spend your last meeting(s) helping your mentee transition to their next voyage. Work with them to set new goals, prepare for new experiences, and identify resources and people who can help them continue to grow.

Occasionally, you will encounter a mentee with whom you have a deeper connection. Perhaps, in them, you see your younger self, aggressively pursuing goals with endless energy and unfiltered ambition. It's not so much that you *want* to help, it's that you are compelled to. If both of you want to continue to learn from each other, then do it! Take time to envision the next phase of your relationship. Establish new goals, guidelines and rhythms. Continue your climb or find a new mountain to challenge.

Finally, as you approach the end of your mentorship, remember to reflect on what *you* have learned. Are you a better mentor as the result of spending time with your mentee? Are you better at having difficult discussions or approaching challenging situations? Have you expanded your own network as a result of working with your mentee, or have you learned to use technologies that were once a mystery? You might have learned that you are a great communicator or you may have discovered that you have room to improve. You might now know that patience is not one of your strengths, and may have come to the realization that you may need to slow down and find ways to adapt to your mentee's pace while still applying positive pressure to help them make progress toward their goals. Through this journey, you have likely learned a lot about yourself. As the experience comes to a close, take time to celebrate, for you've both gained from the process.

"By helping others, you will learn how to help yourselves."
—Aung San Suu Kyi

MENTORING IN ACTION

Crystal is a successful entrepreneur and the president of a growing consulting firm. She has been mentoring college students and small business owners for over twenty years, and believes in the power of paying it forward.

Crystal limits most of her mentoring relationships to one year, with a few exceptions, and then allows her mentees to choose their successors. She says, "Knowing that there is a clear end date, and that they will be choosing their replacements, helps my mentees engage in the entire process."

As the formal mentoring relationship comes to a close, Crystal asks her mentees to make a list of the characteristics they believe are important for a mentee to be successful. Then, she asks her mentees to identify candidates with those characteristics. "My mentees know what it takes to derive the greatest benefit from mentoring, which benefits me because they always introduce me to the most disciplined and motivated candidates. As a result, I've had the pleasure of mentoring generations of mentees who are inextricably linked to each other. I mentored Robin, who referred Ruth, who then found Art, who recommended Tim. The four of them have formed their own 'support group' and a couple of them now have their own mentees. Mentoring is one of my greatest joys."

TRANSITION PLAN

Interview your mentee as a way of reflecting on your collective experience. Then, use the questions to help your mentee prepare for the next phase of their journey. Finally, in Part 2, document your own take-aways and lessons learned.

Part 1: Moving Forward

What have you learned from this mentoring experience?

_____

_____

_____

_____

_____

What would you change if you could do it all over again?

_____

_____

_____

_____

_____

What advice do you have for me as a mentor?

_____

_____

_____

_____

_____

What are your goals moving forward? (What do you want to learn, do or be?)

_____

_____

_____

_____

_____

Who can help you achieve your goals?

_____

_____

_____

_____

_____

What are your next steps?

_____

_____

_____

_____

_____

How can I help you transition?

_____

_____

_____

_____

Part 2: What I've Learned

What have you learned from this mentoring experience?

_____

_____

_____

_____

_____

What would you change if you could do it all over again?

_____

_____

_____

_____

_____

What are your goals for mentoring in the future?

_____

_____

_____

_____

_____

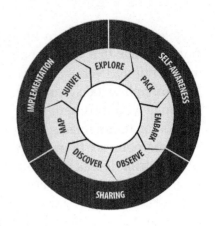

Chapter 9

HANDLING CHALLENGING SITUATIONS

"Smooth seas do not make skillful sailors."
—African Proverb

It's Not Always Easy

Many quotes in this book have been included because they resonate with us. Some we found in books or on the World Wide Web, others we have collected over time holding them for the perfect purpose. But the quote above, "Smooth seas do not make skillful sailors," is uniquely meaningful.

Sometime in 2012 we began working with The American Automobile Association, more commonly known as AAA. They were about to transition to a new customer relationship management system that would replace other legacy software. Software that, although dated and imperfect, was known by everyone in the Organization. Operators knew its flaws and had well-tested workarounds. Programmers understood how to "make it work" from behind the scenes. Was it efficient? Not really. Did it get the job done? Arguably, yes, but that depended on your point of view.

The Company's leadership understood that the system had to be replaced in order to allow the Organization to survive and thrive in the face of a changing environment and growing competition. Our firm,

Metajourn, was hired to help them orchestrate a massive organizational change that would span seven states, impact over 130 branches and continue over three years. We pursued this client engagement with discipline, perseverance and a "we're-not-gonna-quit" attitude – although we almost quit twice.

As you might imagine, navigating this implementation wasn't easy. At some point early in the process, the CIO and project champion, Mike Petrilli, led us to an office on the executive level. The floor was bright and adorned with creative works from local artists representing the best of Florida. The walls were filled with images of wildlife – mostly birds and fish – and with sunny scenes of beaches and marinas. We were assigned a corner office near the door.

Our team would operate out of that office for the better part of a year. We moved in, immediately removed the artwork from the walls, and replaced it with huge sheets of white paper that were ultimately filled with ideas, work flows, plans, and ramblings related to the implementation. We created communications to inform the Organization about the purpose and intent of the change, we brainstormed solutions to address anticipated challenges, and we had candid discussions with those who thought that the lofty goals couldn't be met – especially not in the time frames that had been outlined. Every day there was something unexpected. Every day offered a new obstacle to overcome. Honestly, there were days when we were operating strictly on will.

During that time, our entire team worked tirelessly to help our client achieve their goals. Mike Petrilli became our somewhat unwilling mentor. We would go to him with challenge in hand, and of course a list of possible solutions supported by the pros and cons of each. We won't tell you what he would say when we'd walk in the room with an unanticipated problem that needed to be addressed immediately. Suffice to say that feedback is sometimes harsh and real. But together, we made a pretty incredible team: he, our unwilling mentor, and we, his somewhat-willing mentees.

Through his actions, Mike showed us that if you have an idea that will improve your organization and the lives of those around you, you must pursue it with everything you've got. As the CIO, he could have given up and given in, and left the mountain just as it was, but Mike would never do that. Because Mike Petrilli is perhaps one of the most visionary leaders with whom we've ever had the pleasure of working. There were many very late nights when teams of people – on their side and ours – were working on content to train staff across the U.S. and Mike was right there with us. We'd send files at 2:00 a.m., and he would return them by 3:30 a.m.

After we successfully trained the first two states to use the new system, we moved on to Phase 2 and planned to move out of our executive office. One of the last projects of Phase 1 included creating a communications video to formally launch the system to the rest of the Organization. We shot the video in our office. As we were preparing the set, we realized that it would be enhanced with some artwork. We remembered that we had placed a couple of large pictures behind the bookcases. We pulled them out and hung them on the wall. At exactly that moment, Mike walked through the door.

We looked up and noticed that the massive artwork depicted pirates navigating the roughest seas we had ever seen. They looked like they'd been plucked straight from the Poseidon Adventure, and they were in striking contrast to the sunset-inspired paintings just outside our door. The metaphor was not lost on any of us. Without flinching, Mike looked at the two of us and said, "Smooth seas do not make skillful sailors." That is perhaps the most important thing that either of us has ever learned from a mentor.

Growing a business is not for the faint of heart, any entrepreneur can tell you that. As we navigate the ebbs and flows of business, we often reflect on the day that changed us. We intentionally purchased two works of art depicting smooth seas, and hung them in our main conference room alongside a plaque containing our beloved quote. Thanks to circumstances good and bad, and to our mentors, we are learning to become quite skillful sailors.

Becoming a Skillful Sailor

We would be remiss if we told you that every mentoring relationship will be perfect, and that every meeting will occur as planned. It's best to anticipate the unexpected, and then flex when you need to. That said, we've learned a lot working with thousands of mentors and mentees over the years. What follows is our best advice, in dialogue format, for handling some of the most common and challenging mentoring situations.

"Advice is like snow; the softer it falls, the longer it dwells
upon, and the deeper it sinks into, the mind."
—Samuel Taylor Coleridge

Challenge 1.
"I don't have time"

Mentor: Hey John, how's it going?

Mentee: I'm getting a bit of a groove and everything seems to be going well.

Mentor: Well, good. I was a bit curious because I haven't seen you in a couple of months. You know,   we couldn't meet last month... I know we talked on the phone once, but that was a really brief conversation. So, I was starting to get concerned that you might be needing some help.

Mentee: No no, I'm good. Just busy. You know how things go. There's just a lot to do. And I'm taking care of it, but it's just a lot.

Mentor: Great to hear. So, everything is going well? You're not having time issues, in terms of trying to meet your job duties?

Mentee: Well, I didn't say that. I said everything is getting done. Doesn't mean I'm getting it done like what you are saying. No, there are some things I'm struggling with.

Mentor: That's fair. So, let me tell you something that I'm a bit concerned with [and I will say that I take part of the blame]. As you know, it's my job to support you.

Mentee: I never said you didn't support me.

Mentor: I know, I know, I'm not saying you did. I just want you to know that I take this relationship very seriously. Quite honestly, I learn as much from these interactions as I hope that you are learning too. So, I was a little concerned when we weren't able to get together last month. I want to make sure that I am supporting you and helping you reach the goals that you set for yourself at the beginning of the year.

Mentee: I think you are doing a great job.

Mentor: What I need you to understand is that the meetings are very important to me. So, we need to figure out how we can have more consistent meetings. What do you think is getting in your way of being able to come to our meetings?

Mentee: Well, originally we set these meetings to be the first Monday of the month at 4 o'clock. I thought that would give me enough time to wrap up the day and get to the meeting, but there is always something that comes up. I can never leave when I need to.

Mentor: I totally get it. So, what do you think would be a better time?

Mentee: I have about an hour and a half between when my meeting on Wednesday ends and another begins. That would be the best time.

Mentor: Well, that sounds perfect! So, let's take a look at your calendar and choose a Wednesday that works for you this month.

Mentee: I know that's a bit out of your way, but it would really help me out.

Mentor: Absolutely! Like I said, these meetings are valuable to me and I want to make them work.

Mentee: That would be really helpful.

Mentor: Okay, so, let's look at your calendar and set some dates, and I think for our next meeting we should spend some time talking about time management. Since we'll be at your office, we can go through your calendar tasks and see if there is anything I can help you with.

Mentee: Okay, great. I look forward to our meeting.

Challenge 2.
"Rejection"

Mentor: Hey John, how are you?

Mentee: I'm pretty good.

Mentor: So the last time we talked, you expressed an interest in running a department meeting and you said you'd create an agenda for their next meeting.

Mentee: Yeah, I did.

Mentor: So, did you bring the agenda with you today?

Mentee: No, I didn't. When I talked with my manager she told me that Mike runs the meetings and she didn't see a need for me to do it.

Mentor: Okay, did you talk with her about why you wanted to do it?

Mentee: Yes, I did tell her that you and I had talked about it and that I have an interest in eventually leading a department.

Mentor: Oh good, and what did she say.

Mentee: Basically, she said that I don't really need to run the department meeting and maybe I should think of something else that I'd like to do.

Mentor: Okay, so did you further that conversation with her about what other opportunities might be available to you?

Mentee: I'll be honest, I didn't get the impression that it was a priority to her. I felt the conversation had gone as far as it could go.

Mentor: When you met with her, what was the environment of the office at the time? Was it a quiet time, before lunch, or did she have a meeting to go to?

Mentee: It was after lunch, but you know there's never a good time. Our meeting was interrupted a few times, but I just didn't get the impression that she thought it was something I could do.

Mentor: Well, we also talked last time about the goals she set for you. Did you have a chance to talk to her about how those goals align with the goals you set for yourself?

Mentee: After I got my no on the department meetings, I gave up because I basically got the door shut on me.

Mentor: Well, let's not just totally throw out this opportunity. Have you ever thought of creating your own agenda? It may not be played out in the department meeting, but you could still attend and then go back and compare your agenda to the actual one from the meeting.

Mentee: Yeah, that's actually a good idea. I think I could do that.

Mentor: All right, so let's table this part of the meeting for now. You go back and attend the meeting with your agenda. She didn't say you couldn't attend, right?

Mentee: No, we can attend any meeting we want. She just said that I couldn't run the meeting.

Mentor: Okay, great. So, let's go with this plan. Why don't you attend and after the meeting you create an agenda for the very next meeting. Then, bring it in and we will discuss it together.

Mentee: Would it be all right if I wrote down some strengths of the meeting and maybe some things I think they could improve on?

Mentor: That would be perfect. Before we go, I'd like to touch on something you brought up earlier in the meeting. When you said that your manager didn't want you to run the meeting, did she talk about specifically why?

Mentee: I mean, she just said that Mike was already in charge of it. She also mentioned that I hadn't been in my role very long and that I should focus on learning my job and not try to take on too many other things.

Mentor: Well, that's strong advice and it seems that you heard what she was saying. So, why don't we work on that? I know you said she had some specific things that she wanted you to work on. Could it be that she wanted you to show some initiative and prove to her that you can do some of those things before moving on to other tasks?

Mentee: I can understand that. Let's be real, this isn't the job I'm going to do my entire life. I feel like I am a reasonably intelligent person and I think I can handle more than one thing at a time.

Mentor: And I am sure you can too. Just in the conversations we've had, I can tell that. Maybe it's just that she needs you to prove it to her. So, I think if you work on those things first and show her that you've mastered them, then maybe she will open the door to other opportunities.

Mentee: I think you're right. Hopefully, by attending the meetings, I will be able to get to know the staff better and have some conversations with them and learn about what they are doing.

Mentor: I thing that's a great approach. Thanks, and I really look forward to our next meeting.

Mentee: Me too, thanks for the advice and great ideas.

Challenge 3.
"Avoidance"

(Email sent to the Mentee)

Hi John, it's Susan, your mentor. I've left you a few messages and I sent a few emails, but I haven't heard back from you. I hope you are doing well and enjoying your new position. I would like to set up some time to have our initial meeting. We are a few months behind and we have a lot of things to cover, so the sooner the better. Please give me a call back, so we can set that up. Thanks!

(Two weeks later, break-room encounter)

Mentor: Hey, how's it going?

Mentee: Good.

Mentor: I'm Susan, your mentor. Are you doing all right?

Mentee: I'm doing well, thanks.

Mentor: You've been working here for about two months now... Is everything going okay?

Mentee: Yeah, it's going great.

Mentor: I'm so glad I was able to catch you.

Mentee: Well, I'm just in here grabbing a drink and then I have to go back to my office

Mentor: I was in the neighborhood today and I just wanted to stop by to make sure you and I have a chance to meet because we keep missing each other. I emailed you a couple of times, and we swapped phone calls a couple of times.

Mentee: I appreciate those calls; by the way, they were helpful.

Mentor: I'd really like to be able to sit down with you so we can get the mentoring process started. It's a relationship that we need to make sure we start building.

Mentee: Yes.

Mentor: Okay. Maybe we can set up our first meeting so we can go ahead and start getting to know each other.

Mentee: Sounds good. When do you want to meet?

Mentor: Let's meet this Thursday at 4:00 pm and let's spend some time talking about your goals and what you'd like to get out of the relationship.

Mentee: Okay, great. Will do.

Challenge 4.
"I'm Too Busy"

Mentor: Hey, how are you doing? (Shake hands)

Mentee: Good, how are you?

Mentor: I haven't seen you in a week or two... How are things going?

Mentee: Everything's going great... I'm starting to get settled in.

Mentor: Glad to hear that. Last time we talked about department meetings, and coming in with an agenda that you would have created.

Mentor: Judging by that look, I'm guessing you don't have it?

Mentee: I don't have my agenda with me.

Mentor: Okay... Do you have it – just not with you?

Mentee: No, I didn't have time to make one up.

Mentor: Okay. What happened?

Mentee: Well, you know, I have so many things on my plate, I considered calling you and telling you we couldn't even meet today because I feel like I need to get those cleared.

Mentor: I'm really glad you didn't do that because even though we can't talk about the agenda, we can talk about this a little bit. You're talking about being busy, and trying to get everything done. Time management is a big part of our job. Do you have a plan for the day?

Mentee: I show up to work, and then I take whatever comes at me.

Mentor: Okay... Do you keep a calendar?

Mentee: Yeah, I have a calendar with my lists of things to do.

Mentor: There are some things I think we can talk about here. You're blocking out parts of the day for specific things. What do you do with the time you don't block out?

Mentee: I'm just taking whatever comes at me. You know how it goes.

Mentor: I know… But I'm not here to tell you how to do it; I'm just asking what's keeping you busy.

Mentee: Yeah.

Mentor: Could you take a few minutes to write down what's keeping you from doing the things we talked about? I'm sure there must be more than that that's eating up your time.

Mentee: Sure.

Mentor: Are you done with your list?

Mentee: Yes, I am.

Mentor: Now, here's what I'd like you to do. I'd like for you to go through that list and circle the things that are high priority and need to be done right away. We will call these "execute now" items.

Mentor: Now, I'd like you to put a square around the things that you can plan for later. These are tasks that have a deadline, but do not need to be addressed immediately. For example, preparing a presentation for a staff meeting at the end of the week. After you do that, put a star next to things that can be delegated. These are tasks that need to be taken care of, but that you can assign to others. Finally put a line through the tasks that are time wasters and will only get in the way of your high priority tasks.

Mentee: Okay.

Mentor: Was that list pretty typical, or now that you know we're look-ing at priorities versus delegation, is there anything you'd add now?

Mentee: I could probably spend a bit more time thinking about what I could delegate to someone else.

Mentor: Excellent! By taking a few minutes to prioritize your day you will have more time to focus on what matters most.

Mentor: I'd like for you to complete this prioritizing activity for one full week. At the beginning of each work day list your tasks and then take a moment to prioritize them. Bring your cat-egorized lists with you to our next meeting and we can review them together. Does that sound like a good plan?

Mentee: Sure.

Mentoring in Action

Paula Grand's participation in a one-year leadership development program for women proved to be a turning point in her professional life. The program centered on monthly meetings with 34 other professional women in her area. Each meeting involved a speaker and a timely topic. The women shared stories, discussed challenges, and exchanged strategies for handling common situations related to the topic. Paula enjoyed networking with local business owners and learning from their experiences, but her greatest joy came from participating in the mentoring matching offered in month three of the program.

Although this was not Paula's first mentoring experience, it was her first opportunity to be mentored by a female professional. Paula was paired with Ann Kipling – a strong, successful, and no-nonsense entrepreneur who continues to offer helpful advice, even today. Through the program, Paula began to recognize the subtle, yet significant, ways women hold themselves back. Through the mentoring relationship, she discovered (and learned how to leverage) her personal strengths, which was critical to her continued career growth. Previous relationships had focused more on gaps and developmental needs, so the switch in focus was "a breath of fresh air."

Paula said, "In the past I spent so much time trying to 'fix' what was wrong with me that I lost sight of the things I do well. Ann helped me to focus on my 'gifts' and to learn how to turn them into true assets in the workplace. Honestly, it changed my life and gave me a new-found confidence in my abilities."

Paula is now an active executive mentor, and speaks to new mentees several times a year. She talks to women about the importance of mentoring each other, and encourages them to give back to other women on the rise. "Men tend to do more informal peer mentoring than women," she points out. "Women need to know that it's okay to seek advice from trusted confidants, it's a necessity!"

Paula has also extended her mentoring to young women by partnering with a local university to mentor students who are ready to enter the job market. She helps mentees create compelling résumés, navigate the job search process, prepare for interviews, and dress for success. But she also helps them negotiate job offers and build their professional networks. "How you begin your career, from a financial aspect, can influence where you end up later in your career. Research shows that men are generally more confident when negotiating salaries and benefits, while women often don't want to 'rock the boat'. I think it's important for young women to become their own best advocates. I try to share all the lessons I wish I'd known when I was starting out."

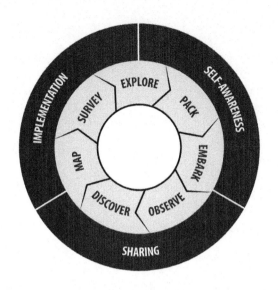

Part 2

FOR THE MENTEE

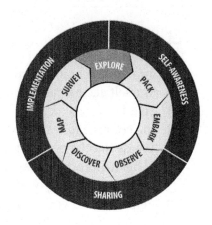

Chapter 10

EXPLORE: INTROSPECTION

"Never give advice. Just use yourself and your experiences as a 'been there, done that' model."
—Louis Schmier, Valdosta State University

So You Want to Become a Mentee?

A mentee is a person who is advised or counseled by a mentor. If you feel that you are doing all that you can, but you've hit a wall, then you might want to become a mentee. If you are ready to advance in your career or are considering a career change, you might want to become a mentee. If you are ambitious, but feel that you've hit a plateau, you might want to become a mentee. If you are at a place in your career or your life where you think you could benefit from any of the following, then you might want to become a mentee:

- ❏ Help defining your long-term goals
- ❏ Help developing a plan to achieve your long-term goals
- ❏ Guidance and direction without control
- ❏ A confidant and trusted advisor
- ❏ A stronger, more robust network of the "right" connections
- ❏ Someone else's experience and perspective
- ❏ Out-of-the-box thinking

- ❏ Inspiration
- ❏ Emotional support
- ❏ Someone to hold you accountable and who could help you hold yourself accountable
- ❏ An ally
- ❏ The courage to take risks
- ❏ Access to others who may be in a position to help you
- ❏ A "been there done that" approach to working through challenges
- ❏ Someone to help you develop your brand
- ❏ Help building your confidence
- ❏ Help understanding and navigating through your workplace culture
- ❏ A role model for your career journey

A mentor can help you stand out among your peers, and can give you the edge you need to reach your career aspirations. Mentoring is, without a doubt, a privilege for both the mentee and the mentor, but with privilege comes responsibility. Mentoring involves explicit agreements between a mentor and a mentee that can ultimately result in a mutually beneficial partnership. As a mentee, you will need to be open to feedback, patient with the process, gracious to your mentor, and considerate of their time. You will need to actively engage in the mentoring process and will want to collaborate with your mentor to advance your career. Although your mentor may initially take the lead in the relationship, the long-term success of the partnership will ultimately lie with you.

Not surprisingly, the people who benefit the most from mentoring are often ambitious, driven, eager to learn, self-aware, and a bit humble. In other words, they understand that they don't know everything, and are open to learning from others. While those at the opposite end of the spectrum – people who are overly confident in their own abilities – could fail to derive substantial benefits from a mentoring relationship, especially if they are resistant to advice from others with more experience and expertise.

The "right" mentor – in the "right" situation – can help you accelerate your career and avoid pitfalls along the way. A mentor can help you select a path that aligns with your true career aspirations, and can help you consider alternate paths to the achievement of your goals. The "right" mentor will also work hard to help you identify potential blind spots that could be hindering your success, and may also help you overcome limiting beliefs. They will sometimes challenge you with feedback that you might not be prepared to hear, but the best mentors will always act with your interests at heart.

Your mentor will support you, make observations, offer insights and guidance. And you will be the benefactor. But they, too, have a lot to gain from the relationship. Some mentors benefit from the satisfaction of helping someone else traverse the corporate world. Others are driven by helping their organizations retain high-potential employees. While others enjoy counseling mentees as a way to give back or leave a legacy.

Mentors also benefit from the exchange of information. For example, retired executives, willing to share their expertise, can speak to the road to the executive suite. But they can also learn about navigating a "new" company with a flatter organizational structure. Likewise, through mentoring, mentors can stay relevant. We recently heard from veteran mentors who have learned about technology from their younger mentees. The best mentoring relationships involve two-way information sharing, which builds the capacity of both the mentor and the mentee. If you enter into a mentoring relationship looking for ways you can support or assist your mentor, rather than just expecting valuable advice to be handed over unconditionally, the mutual experience should be gratifying.

Finding the Mentor You Need

Just because you want a mentor does not necessarily mean that you are ready for one. Before you go on a quest to find someone who can help, take some time to understand your motivations and your needs. Answering the following questions can help to narrow your search and point you in the right direction:

- ☐ What do you want from a mentor?
- ☐ What kind of mentor do you think you need?
- ☐ How do you think a mentor can help you?
- ☐ Are your expectations for a mentoring relationship realistic?
- ☐ Do you have ample time to commit to working with a mentor?
- ☐ How can you help a mentor?

There are other important questions to ask about a potential mentor – questions that extend beyond technical skills and career aspirations. A compatible relationship requires a personal connection. Although that's not to say that you have to have similar personalities or interests in order for the relationship to work. It simply means that you need to have the capacity for a harmonious and productive partnership. When seeking out a mentor, keep the following questions in mind:

- ☐ Do you genuinely like the person?
- ☐ Can you picture the individual being your mentor?
- ☐ Do you respect the person's experience and perspective?
- ☐ Could you learn from them?
- ☐ Could you trust the person with confidential or sensitive information?
- ☐ Do the two of you have chemistry?
- ☐ If this person were to tell you something you didn't really want to hear, would you be able to learn from their advice?

If the answer to any of these questions is "no," then keep looking. You might be a perfect match in terms of skills and background, but if you don't think you can comfortably reveal personal information about your goals and career plans, then this isn't the right mentor for you. When it comes to mentoring, chemistry trumps even a perfect match of talents or position.

Insider or Outsider?

So, you've determined that you're ready to be a mentee. In fact, by now, you have probably even defined the characteristics you're looking for in a mentor. Now, it's time to find one! But where do you look?

If your goal is to climb the corporate ladder or to navigate the corporate matrix, you might look for someone inside your organization that is at least two positions above you – someone who has previously travelled the road you hope to take. If your goal is to make a lateral move into another area of the company, you might consider being mentored by a colleague who has successfully made a similar transition. A mentor inside your company can help because they will likely:

- Know the corporate culture and the senior managers, and will be in a position to advise you on how best to achieve your goals given the corporate dynamic.

- Be aware of upcoming managerial or staffing changes that could present you with new opportunities.

- Be able to become your champion within the company.

- Be in a position to help you network and build relationships within the company.

- Be in a position to understand how you are perceived by others in the Organization.

If your company or association has a formal mentoring program, you can get some assistance in finding a good match. These programs generally offer training and resources for both the mentor and mentee, and pair mentors and mentees at no cost.

But mentors can also be found outside your organization. If you are considering a career change, you might look for someone who holds a job you're interested in or who is working in your target industry. If you have political aspirations, you might want to connect with someone who holds a prominent position in the public sector. Some of the advantages to having a mentor who is employed outside your current company include:

- An outside mentor may be able to be more objective, forming their opinions based on what they have personally witnessed rather than being affected by the impressions of others.

- They may be more objective about your career possibilities and may offer a creative approach to reaching your goals.

- They may have a broader network with whom you can connect and learn from.

- You may feel more comfortable opening up to someone who may be less likely to leak sensitive information to your boss or colleagues; trust may come more easily.

- The advice you receive may be based more on the strengths you display than on the company's hiring and professional development needs.

When determining whether to look for a mentor inside or outside your current employer, take your goals into account. If your goal is to become the CEO, you probably want to connect with people of prominence in your own company and find ways to make a name for yourself internally. However, if you are open to broader opportunities outside your current employer and hope to rise within your industry or within another industry altogether, then consider searching for a mentor outside the company walls.

Choosing Your Mentor Wisely

Although you might be eager to be paired with a mentor, be careful not to jump into a mentoring relationship that is not a good fit. One could argue that having no mentor is better than having a mentor who isn't right for you. The wrong mentor can slow your progress, waste your time, and even derail your career. So don't rush. Resist the temptation to jump at the first opportunity or offer, because you may miss out when an even better choice arises.

As you consider potential mentors, there are some you may want to avoid, including:

- **Your direct supervisor.** Sure, it may sound like a good idea, initially. But in general, it's not. For starters, you should look for a mentor with whom you can be completely honest, and at times even emotional. Although your boss may be kind and empathetic, transparency with the person who is completing your performance appraisal can be risky. Secondly, you could find yourself competing with your supervisor for a project or a position. No matter who gets the role, the process could be awkward. If your manager has something to teach you, then learn from them, but do your best to avoid entering into a mentoring relationship.

- **The mentor under duress.** Most prospective mentors volunteer to be part of a formal or informal corporate mentoring program because they enjoy advising and supporting others. Occasionally, people are pushed into mentoring begrudgingly. Keep your eye out for someone who is motivated and willing to dedicate time to mentoring. Walk away from someone who is mentoring because they were told to.

- **The understaffed manager.** Some mentors are really only in it for their own good, and you'll know this when they start asking about your availability and willingness to pitch in as needed on projects they're involved in. Chances are good you will soon be asked to take on additional work for no additional pay or recognition. This is not a mentoring relationship, nor will you likely receive equal time with your "mentor" in exchange for your hard work. So, again, offer a polite "Thank you," and walk away.

- **The mentor with whom you have no chemistry.** You may find someone who looks great on paper, with all of the knowledge and experience you're looking for in a mentor. However, if you feel the slightest bit uneasy or uncomfortable around a potential mentor, this individual is not for you. The biggest determinant of a successful mentoring relationship is the ability to quickly develop a level of trust. If you don't click with a prospective mentor, don't settle. Keep looking.

Although you may be in a rush to find a mentor, committing to work with someone who happens to be available may turn out to be a huge disappointment and a complete waste of time. Backing out of such a relationship could be extremely awkward, and may be perceived as unprofessional by those around you. So, don't jump in headfirst. Approach finding a mentor as carefully as you would approach finding your next job.

Beginning the Hunt

If your organization offers a mentoring program, you might want to start there. Although you might not find your perfect match, it's worth entering your name and information to see the kind of candidates who come forward.

But don't limit yourself when starting your search for a mentor. You might find a match through an industry association, local trade group or your alma mater. Ask around to find groups that match mentees with volunteer mentors. Some career counseling companies will also match you with a mentor for a fee. Don't immediately discount this option, especially if you are in search of specialized expertise.

If you already have a list of people you'd like to have as a mentor, a third option is to reach out to them personally to ask if they would consider serving as your mentor. Before making contact, make sure the individuals on your wish list can support your career goals. You should be interested in working with them because of their track record, not their celebrity. You may impress your colleagues by being able to claim your CEO as your mentor, but if your goals include starting your own business, you'd be better off being mentored by a successful entrepreneur.

Before you approach any of your "dream team" mentors, try to find out first how they'd like to be approached. Don't just walk into their office unannounced and try to strike up a conversation. It won't work. Instead, ask for advice from people who know them well. Would your top mentor candidate prefer a phone call, email or personal note? Is there anything you can say that might make them more likely to agree to a mentorship? For example, would the fact that you grew up in the same town, went to the same school, worked for a certain manager, etc., win any points? You never know, and it can't hurt to ask or do some research.

While you may have several people in mind as mentors, start with just one and see how that relationship develops, before you seek out a second or a third. Having multiple mentors with different skill sets can be useful in some cases, if they can help in different ways. For example, if you want to enter the real estate market, it might be helpful to find a mentor who is a successful broker in your area. At the same time, if you are hoping to grow your real estate business through social media, you might find an expert in that area. But keep in mind: mentoring requires time and dedication from both parties. If you decide to take on multiple mentors, do so with caution.

A really good mentor can be hard to find. When you do find one, do your best to protect and respect your relationship. Your mentor can be your best champion and may provide observations and insights that could affect the course of your future.

With that said, be advised that even the best laid plans can go awry. If you enter into a mentorship with the best of intentions, but months later are struggling to connect with your mentor, don't stick with the relationship hoping this will change. Go with your gut. If, after a few meetings, you know that your mentor is not the right match for you, then make a change. Either talk to your company's mentorship coordinator or simply be honest with your mentor. Take the lead and find a mentor who is a better fit.

The Mentee Self-Assessment

We developed the Mentee Self-Assessment (on the pages that follow) to help you zero in on your goals and find the type of mentor who can best help you achieve them. The easiest way to find a good mentor is to consider your strengths and weaknesses, and to determine what you hope to accomplish. A self-assessment can help you:

- Identify your greatest opportunities for improvement

- Remind you of how you got to where you are, and which skills have aided your career path

- Confirm or readjust your career plan after recognizing your true strengths and weaknesses

- Spot communication preferences and patterns that can aid or interfere with your new mentoring relationship

With introspection, you'll be able to identify your needs and communicate those needs to your mentor. If your mentor understands your strengths, weaknesses and current work situation, they will be in a position to offer effective career guidance. For example, if your self-assessment reveals that negotiating is an area where you could use some additional training or coaching, you will want to share that with your mentor. After all, what if one of your first homework assignments is to begin to negotiate a pay raise? You're currently not in the best position to do that and your mentor needs to know. Share what you recognize about yourself so that your mentor can more quickly get to know you and help you.

It's also important to consider the characteristics of a mentor who is likely to be a good fit for you as a mentee. Use the list contained in the Mentee Self-Assessment to consider your preferences. Then, share that list with your mentor. Talk about why these characteristics are important to you, and ask what is important to them in a mentee. The conversation can be a helpful way for you to get to know each other.

MENTORING IN ACTION

"I graduated with a master's degree in education, and quickly found a teaching position. Like many other aspiring educators, my goal was to change the entire educational system for the better," said Sam Roth. "No doubt, I had high expectations.

"As a first-year teacher, I was paired with a mentor charged with helping me acclimate to the job. Looking back, I'd say that I was a fairly unwilling participant. The truth is I was so focused on rising through the administrative ranks that I failed to give appropriate attention to my role as a teacher. As a result, my first year was – by all accounts – an epic fail."

Sam shared that although he went through the mentoring process, it was all pretty mechanical. He met regularly with his mentor. They chatted about events and challenges, but his attention was generally elsewhere. He was focused on increasing his visibility, and moving toward his ultimate goal of becoming the District Superintendent.

"One day, my very skilled mentor told me the truth. She said, 'Sam, you're a great guy with high aspirations. I think that someday, you might make a great administrator. But today, you are a teacher. And a teacher is, frankly, the most important position in the District. If you lose sight of the kids, you lose of sight of everything.' I still remember those words today."

Since then, Sam has had many mentors, and has mentored countless mentees. But now, every time he enters into a mentoring relationship, he takes an inventory of his goals, his strengths, and his challenges. He consciously sets his ego aside and commits to "focusing on today with an eye toward the future." He said, "My mantra is, 'Be here now.' It's simple, but it keeps me grounded and focused on what's important. I encourage my mentees to think the same way."

Sam has successfully risen through the ranks of administration, and he is – by all accounts -- changing education for the better. Today, he is an advocate for his district and sits on numerous national committees. He is also a frequent speaker on trends in education, reminding anyone who will listen that teachers are the ones with the power to impact the lives and futures of our children.

MENTEE SELF-ASSESSMENT

What Talents Do You Want to Develop?

Check the boxes next to the talents that you would like to develop through mentoring.

Talents Checklist

- ☐ Adaptability
- ☐ Analytical thinking
- ☐ Coaching
- ☐ Counseling
- ☐ Command presence
- ☐ Communication
- ☐ Creativity
- ☐ Developing people
- ☐ Empathy
- ☐ Empowering others
- ☐ Flexible thinking
- ☐ Influencing others
- ☐ Leadership
- ☐ Listening

- ☐ Managing conflict
- ☐ Managing people
- ☐ Motivating others
- ☐ Negotiating
- ☐ Networking
- ☐ Problem solving
- ☐ Self-motivated
- ☐ Strategy
- ☐ Team dynamics
- ☐ Visionary
- ☐ Other:
- ☐ Other:
- ☐ Other:
- ☐ Other:

List your Top 5 Priorities below.

1._____

2._____

3._____

4._____

5._____

How will these talents contribute to your long-term career success?

_____

_____

_____

_____

_____

What Skills Do You Want to Develop?

Check the boxes next to the skills you would like to develop through mentoring.

Skills Checklist

- ☐ Administrative
- ☐ Analytics
- ☐ Budgeting
- ☐ Business development
- ☐ Business solutions
- ☐ Career planning
- ☐ Computer
- ☐ Cost management
- ☐ Decision making
- ☐ Interpersonal
- ☐ Interviewing
- ☐ Market development
- ☐ Marketing
- ☐ Organizing

- ☐ Prioritizing
- ☐ Planning
- ☐ Presentation
- ☐ Project management
- ☐ Recruiting
- ☐ Time management
- ☐ Training
- ☐ Writing
- ☐ Other:
- ☐ Other:
- ☐ Other:
- ☐ Other:
- ☐ Other:
- ☐ Other:

List your Top 5 Priorities below.

1._____

2._____

3._____

4._____

5._____

How will these talents contribute to your long-term career success?

_____

_____

_____

_____

_____

Mentor Match

Understanding what you are hoping to accomplish through a mentorship can help you find the "right" mentor. Examine your goals and objectives by answering the questions below.

1. What do you think a mentor can do for you?
2. What would you like to learn from your mentor?
3. What are your short-term job objectives?
4. What do you expect to contribute to the mentoring process?

Comments:

_____

_____

_____

_____

_____

_____

What qualities and characteristics are you looking for in a mentor?

- ❏ Passion – Has a positive attitude and is enthusiastic about mentoring
- ❏ Generosity – Actively supports your development; is not threatened by your success
- ❏ Reputation – Is well-respected by others
- ❏ Competency – Knowledge and experience in areas that are important to me
- ❏ Availability – Has ample time to dedicate to mentoring
- ❏ Self-awareness – Willingness to share knowledge and expertise
- ❏ Honesty – Provides guidance and constructive feedback
- ❏ Openness – Seeks the ideas and opinions of others
- ❏ Discretion – Maintains confidences; is trustworthy
- ❏ Connectedness – Has a robust network and strong connections
- ❏ Communication – Keeps in touch; regularly shares information
- ❏ Compatibility – Ability to work well together
- ❏ Reliability – Keeps promises and commitments
- ❏ Specificity – Provides directions and detailed advice
- ❏ Similarity – Held your position of interest or took the path you plan to take
- ❏ Other:
- ❏ Other:
- ❏ Other:

List your goals for the mentoring relationship.

1._____

2._____

3._____

Potential Mentors:

1._____

2._____

3._____

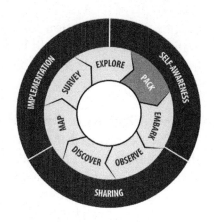

Chapter 11

PACK: GATHER INFORMATION

"The greatest good you can do for another is not just to share your riches, but to reveal to him his own."
—Benjamin Disraeli

Finding the Right Mentor

You reflected on your long-term career goals. You thought about your strengths and weaknesses. You identified the talents and skills you want to develop through mentorship. You're ready to find a mentor! While they say there is only one perfect soul mate for each of us, there are many potential mentors who can help you achieve your personal and career goals. You simply need to find the right match for you.

Keep in mind that every mentoring relationship is unique. Someone who might be your perfect pairing may be a poor choice for one of your colleagues. The "right" mentor will have had the work experiences you would like to have, will have held a position you aspire to hold, will have specific skills and abilities you would like to develop, will have a reputation you admire, and will hopefully have the time and interest to mentor you.

Time and interest are critical characteristics of a good mentor match. A skilled mentor lacking the right motivation probably won't be a good fit for you. Someone who volunteered to mentor under duress, or as a qualification for some honor or role, may not be a good match for you. You should look for a mentor who is more interested in helping you succeed than they are in helping themselves look good.

Considering Your Options

If you completed the Mentee Self-Assessment in Chapter 10, you should have a list of the skills and talents you would like to develop, and an idea about the goals you'd like to pursue with support from your mentor. Those insights can inform conversations with mentor candidates and can help you identify those who may be a match. Being clear about your own needs and aspirations can aid in finding potential mentors who are strong where you are weak, and who have the career experiences you aspire to.

Although the Mentee Self-Assessment is a good place to start, don't shy away from other surveys and tools that can help you learn more about yourself. If you have access to a formal mentoring program through your employer or an association to which you belong, ask to participate. Going through the process of completing the application, answering questions about the type of mentor you would like, and being matched with someone from their database could be a useful exercise. Worst case, you'll be matched with someone who isn't a good fit, in which case you can politely decline. Through the process, though, you will learn something about yourself and may discover how your responses on the application led to the "wrong" match. The feedback could help you adjust or refine the description of the mentor you hope to find.

Another benefit of applying to a formal mentoring program is that you'll expend less time and energy chasing potential mentors who may have no interest in the process, and you may be able to quickly initiate a mentoring relationship once a match is made. Who knows, you may be matched with the perfect mentor who can help you learn and grow – perhaps someone you hadn't previously considered.

Visualizing Your Perfect Mentor

The best way to find a mentor who aligns with your goals, personality, work ethic, communication style, and ambition is to have a clear picture of the person's characteristics. Don't try to picture what they look like in person. Let's face it, your ideal mentor could be a man or a woman, young or old; that's not what's important. Instead, your ideal mentor should be well suited to support the achievement of your goals. So, consider the following when describing your perfect mentor:

- Current position

- Current business unit, functional area or industry

- Current employer

- Educational level

- Years of work experience

- Career path/background

- Career aspirations

- Skills

- Social network

- Personal interests

- Family life

You'll also want to keep your goals and unique requirements in mind when conducting your search. For example, if one of your goals is to continue to climb the career ladder while raising small children, you may want to consider a mentor who has a young family and maintains a senior-level position at work. If destiny calls you to work on the operations side of your company, but all your experience has been in accounting, you might benefit from a mentor who has transitioned into operations from another department. In short, if you know where you want to go, you can probably find someone else who has already been there.

Doing Your Homework

If you already have an idea of the characteristics you are looking for in a mentor, take some time to develop a list of potential candidates. The list can include people you already know; people you know of, but don't have a relationship with; and people others may recommend. Once you have a list of three, five or ten potential mentors, do some research and learn more about them. Talk with people who know them and ask what they are like. Find out if they have mentored other people in the past. Then, search the internet for as much information as you can find.

These days, there is an electronic fingerprint for almost everyone in the world. A simple Google search might lead you to an article your potential mentor has written, or one that was written about them. You might find video of a speech or talk that can give you a better sense of who they are and what they stand for. Are they serious or funny? Are they opinionated or light-hearted? Are they energetic or mild-mannered? Do they appear to be introverted or extroverted? Look to their social media profiles to see how they describe themselves, their careers, and the businesses and organizations they're involved in. Find out where they donate money and where they spend their free time. This could help you get a sense of their interests and passions, and could help you determine whether a potential mentor might be a good fit for you. Granted, there is no guarantee that any of the potential mentors on your list will agree to a mentorship, but if you know something about them, you'll show that you've done your homework and have invested some time in finding just the right person to help you on your journey. We've listed some websites, search engines, social media sites, and apps to get you started:

- **Corporate websites.** If you work for a large to mid-size company, you can start by looking at the corporate biographies of senior leaders posted on your company's website. Although these bios are often brief and company focused, they will sometimes contain details about an individual's career path. Take a few moments to analyze the organization chart to see the relationships between key leaders and managers. Map their career paths to see whether they followed a career ladder or whether they took a non-traditional route to the top. Has your potential mentor's journey been similar to the approach you are taking or hope to take? Also, look to see who is on the Board of Directors. Board members often know a lot about the company, although they don't typically hold a position within it. They could be retired execs with a wealth of information, or leaders in other organizations who could help. Again, read the bios of any who may interest you.

- **Search engines (Google, Bing, etc.).** As we mentioned, you can use Google or another search engine to gain access to more public information than you probably want or need. You can learn about previous employers, previous positions, personal interests, volunteer work and much more for each of your candidates.

- **Social Media (Facebook, Instagram, Twitter, etc.).** Facebook is a common networking tool that blends business and personal news. Viewing a potential mentor's status updates could provide clues to their priorities and interests. You can also see a list of any friends you may have in common. Instagram allows photo and video sharing and provides information similar to Facebook. Twitter allows registered users to connect with others in 140 characters or less. Reviewing past tweets posted by potential mentors gives you another look into what issues they routinely grapple with. What topics are of greatest interest to them? What news do they routinely share? Is this in sync with your interests and motivation?

- **LinkedIn.** LinkedIn describes themselves as "The World's Largest Professional Network." This service allows you to make business connections and to learn about individuals in a professional online setting. LinkedIn will show you if others in your network are connected to any of your potential mentors. You can also use LinkedIn to request introductions to people you'd like to know more about.

- **YouTube.** This site offers the ability to create and share videos. Companies are using it more to educate their customers about products and services. If your mentor candidates frequently use social media, you might find videos in which they share their expertise.

Approaching a Potential Mentor

If you are fortunate enough to work for an organization with a formal mentoring program, finding a match may be automated and fairly simple. However, if your company doesn't offer such a benefit, or you are choosing to search on your own, it's important to narrow your choices and then actively pursue candidates at the top of your list.

If you have narrowed your list to high-profile, highly accomplished individuals, you may find also that they are in great demand as mentors. In other words, you might have competition for the coveted spot of mentee. But don't give up…instead, prepare before you approach!

Studies show that people who are successful generally choose to mentor other successful people. So, think about ways you can position yourself as someone who is motivated, determined, and equipped to accomplish their goals. It's better to position yourself as a junior executive-on-the-rise than an underperforming associate in need of guidance. Mentors will invest their time and energy in you. They will share their secrets to achievement, and will expect that you will act on their recommendations. Therefore, if you are looking for a highly desirable mentor, you need to be a highly desirable mentee.

Positioning Yourself for Success

To start, make sure that you are truly motivated, that you can commit to work hard, and that you are willing to stretch beyond your comfort zone. Then, reflect on your strengths and pursue your potential mentor with all the confidence of a skyrocketing new star. Of course, you will want to be honest and authentic. If you're not, you'll be quickly found out by any savvy professional.

To capture a potential mentor, you'll need to attract their attention with a bit of self-packaging. Consider preparing assets that reflect your personal brand. These items can, and should, evolve over time as you take on new projects, develop new skills, and grow in your career. Your initial brand package might include:

- **An updated résumé that showcases your abilities and accomplishments.** Emphasize your achievements rather than your education or volunteer activities (unless, of course, you share an alma mater with a potential mentor).

- **A compelling cover letter that highlights recent successes and describes why the particular individual is well-suited to help you.** Consider mentioning results you've achieved, honors and recognition you've received, career aspirations, and positive performance reviews.

- **A positive online presence.** If potential mentors Googled you, what would they find? Are your LinkedIn, Facebook, and Twitter profiles professional? Are they current? Would a potential mentor be impressed by some of your online colleagues, or would they find slightly scandalous photos of you on spring break a couple of years ago? Make some changes, if necessary, to make sure your online presence reflects the characteristics of a career climber. You should also secure a personal website, if your name as a URL is available. A simple personal website might only contain a brief bio, but it can be a simple way to communicate your brand.

- **References at-the-ready.** Although finding a mentor isn't like applying for a new job, positive references and testimonials from others could sway a mentor on the fence. Gather positive endorsements from colleagues, clients, and previous managers and ask permission to include their contact information in your cover letter.

Your First Contact

An invitation to meet with a potential mentor may arrive during a brief conversation, via phone or email. When the invitation arrives, you should certainly accept. While this may be a sign that your desired mentor is considering mentoring you, approach it much like you would a job interview. Be prepared to answer questions, and to ask questions of your own. Before you commit to a mentorship of any length, you both need to feel confident that you can be a well-suited match. Some questions you may want to pose to your mentor candidate include:

- Why do you want to be a mentor?

- How do you think I can benefit from your counsel and experience?

- Are there specific skills you feel particularly qualified to help develop in me?

- Have you mentored others?

- How have you benefited from mentoring?

- What have you learned from being a mentor?

- Where do you think I have the most potential for growth?

- What do you see as my weaknesses?

- What challenges do you think I face in reaching my career goals?

- What expectations do you have for the mentorship?

- Do you have enough time to devote to mentoring me?

Once you meet with a potential mentor, reflect on your discussion. Consider their responses to your questions. Then, be honest with yourself. Often, mentees will agree to be mentored because the offer itself is flattering, but flattery will quickly wear off with unmet expectations. Resist the temptation to jump at the first opportunity to be mentored, especially if you don't think the person is a good fit. Here are some questions to ask yourself.

- Does the candidate truly want to be a mentor?

- Do they have adequate time to mentor me?

- Do I like them?

- Do I respect them?

- Would I value their advice?

- Would I be comfortable sharing sensitive or confidential information with this person?

- Can I trust them with sensitive information?

- Am I confident they will be honest with me?

- Are our expectations for the relationship well aligned?

- Am I excited about working with this person?

- Would I be proud to call them my mentor?

If the answer to most of these questions is "yes," then you probably found a good mentor. If, on the other hand, you have major reservations, it's best to politely thank your potential mentor and continue your search.

But if you're only slightly unsure about the mentorship, consider a follow-up conversation. You might want to ask a few more questions and share your concerns in hopes of moving forward. Remember, you aren't looking for someone just like you, and you aren't looking for the "perfect" mentor. You are looking, instead, for someone who has been where you want to go. You are looking for someone who is candid, yet caring. But most of all, you are looking for someone who wants you to succeed, and who can help to guide you on your path to achieving your goals. Once you and your mentor agree that you have found a good fit, quickly set a date for your first formal meeting.

Preparing for Your First Meeting

The initial meeting with your mentor should be one part introduction, and one part laying the groundwork to help you achieve your goals. During this important time, you will want to be prepared to share information about yourself, and to learn a lot about the person who has agreed to counsel you. It's as much an opportunity for your mentor to learn all about you, as it is for you to determine how best to tap into your mentor's expertise, network and advice. Use your time to learn more about how your mentor works, how they like to communicate, and how comfortable they are sharing personal experiences.

To prepare for the meeting, take time to educate yourself about your mentor. Read their bio to learn about their current responsibilities, major accomplishments, and most notable qualities. The more you learn before your initial one-on-one, the less time you'll need to spend sharing basic facts. Get that out of the way before you connect with your mentor, and use your valuable time to gain a deeper insight into their experiences and motivations. Through discovery, you might find out:

- Where your mentor went to college

- What they studied

- What degrees they have

- What jobs they held

- What companies they worked for

- What type of reputation they have – good or bad

- What strengths and unique skills they're known for

- What hobbies and interests they pursue

- Which causes or charities they support

- How they have been recognized in the industry or community

- What awards or accolades they have received

- With whom they are aligned and with whom they may be adversarial

With a few facts in hand, prepare a list of questions that you can use to facilitate a discussion with your mentor. Your list may include questions about their career path, and the choices they made along the way. You might ask about education or training they found helpful, and opportunities that might not have been as beneficial as they hoped. You could ask about lessons learned, or advice they might have for someone in your position. Formulating questions in advance will help you stay focused, and will demonstrate your interest in your mentor and your commitment to the process.

In addition to doing research and preparing to learn more about your mentor, think about the information you'd like to share about yourself. Perhaps you'd like to talk about your own strengths and weaknesses, and hear your mentor's perspective on how they might play out in your career of choice. Or you might want to talk about your background and career aspirations as a way of uncovering similarities and differences. Or maybe you'd like to share some facts about your upbringing to help your mentor understand and appreciate your intentions and motivations. By openly sharing information, you will help your mentor offer relevant and sound advice early in the relationship.

Understanding Each Other's Roles

Laying the groundwork for mentoring involves setting clear expectations, discussing roles and responsibilities, and outlining some initial ground rules for the relationship. Although your mentor will be responsible for guiding you as you embark on the mentoring journey, that doesn't mean that you should sit back and expect your mentor to manage the relationship. As a mentee, you need to take responsibility for ensuring that you get what you need. Mentoring isn't coaching. It's not about mastering a specific skill. There is no superior and no subordinate distinction. Instead, mentoring is about working toward longer-term objectives related to personal or career aspirations, where the mentor provides advice, support and counsel.

The amount of time each of you will devote to this relationship, and to your career growth, should also be negotiated up front to ensure that you and your mentor are in sync. If you enter the relationship planning to devote two hours a month to mentoring, yet your mentor thinks you should be allocating more of your time, both of you will likely be disappointed. So, work it out early to avoid future conflicts or misunderstandings.

Mentoring is a two-way street. What you put into the relationship will likely correlate with what you get in return. Begin with a shared understanding, good communication, and a commitment to results, and you will be off to a good start.

MENTORING IN ACTION

For her entire business career, Dana Quest had admired Tom, the CEO of a Fortune 500 company, who makes a regular appearance on the Forbes list of *The Richest People in America*. Although she had never met him, she had followed his career, studying how he grew a small, private payroll processing company into a successful, public company with thousands of customers and employees. Dana's own company was not yet publicly traded, but she had ambitions and dreams that seemed to parallel his. In order to achieve her growth goals, however, she recognized she needed the advice and guidance of someone who had already walked that path...someone like Tom.

Tom was from Dana's home town, so she knew a number of his friends and acquaintances. She attempted to use her connections to get an introduction, but arranging a meeting proved challenging. One day, Dana was working on her vision board with a colleague. As they sorted through pictures and words to adhere to their boards, her colleague noticed that Dana had included meeting Tom on her wish list. The next day, Dana arrived in her office to find a newspaper announcement that said Tom would be speaking at a local event the following week.

Dana went to the event, determined to meet Tom. At the conclusion of the event, Dana, summoning all her courage, walked over, and introduced herself. After a polite exchange, Dana asked for a meeting. To her surprise and delight, Tom responded, "Call my office at 8:30 tomorrow morning and we'll set something up." With this, Dana began a mentoring relationship that has ultimately transformed her business.

When asked about the experience, Dana said, "One thing I've learned is that you can't be shy. If your gut tells you to do something, you should do it. The other thing that I've learned is that there is no substitute for experience. You can read all the books in the world, attend the best seminars, and get the best education that money can buy. But in the end, advice from someone who has been there is priceless!

MENTEE'S PACKING LIST

When planning for a trip, a packing list can help you think about what you need to bring, make sure you are prepared to travel, and serve as a checklist to ensure that your items return home with you at the end of your journey. Likewise, the Mentee's Packing List can help you plan for an initial meeting with your mentor, develop a plan to make best use of your time, and provide a place to capture thoughts and insights from your meeting.

Part 1: Planning and Preparation

(Complete this section prior to your initial meeting.)
Answer the questions below to develop a Mentor Profile.

- What is your mentor's current position?

- Where do they work (business unit or functional area)?

- What is their level of education?

- How long has the person been with the organization or been pursuing their dream role?

- What are their career aspirations?

- What are their goals?

- What are their skills?

- What are their social circles?

- What are their personal interests?

Who is your ideal mentor? Summarize your Mentor's Profile here:

_____

_____

_____

_____

_____

What questions will you ask a potential mentor?
(Check all that apply).

❑ Why do you want to be a mentor?

❑ How do you think I can benefit from your counsel and experience?

❑ Are there specific skills you feel particularly qualified to help develop in me?

❑ Have you mentored others?

❑ How have you benefited from mentoring?

❑ What have you learned from being a mentor?

❑ Where do you think I have the most potential for growth?

❑ What do you see as my weaknesses?

❑ What challenges do you think I face in reaching my career goals?

❑ What expectations do you have for the mentorship?

❑ Do you have enough time to devote to mentoring me?

Part 2: Mentor Candidate Evaluation

Evaluate your initial impressions of the mentor candidate and summarize below.

Mentor Candidate: _____   Title: _____

Question to Evaluate the Candidate	Circle your response.		
Does the mentor candidate truly want to be a mentor?	Yes	No	Unsure
Do they have adequate time to mentor me?	Yes	No	Unsure
Do I like them?	Yes	No	Unsure
Do I respect them?	Yes	No	Unsure
Would I value their advice?	Yes	No	Unsure

Would I be comfortable sharing sensitive information with this person?	Yes	No	Unsure
Can I trust them with sensitive information?	Yes	No	Unsure
Am I confident they will be honest with me?	Yes	No	Unsure
Are our expectations for the relationship well aligned?	Yes	No	Unsure
Am I excited about working with this person?	Yes	No	Unsure
Would I be proud to call them my mentor?	Yes	No	Unsure

Overall impression:

_____

_____

_____

_____

_____

_____

This mentor is a good fit for me. (Circle one.)

Yes   No   Unsure

If yes, we have scheduled an initial meeting for: ___/___/___

Evaluate your initial impressions of the mentor candidate and summarize below.

Mentor Candidate: _____   Title: _____

Question to Evaluate the Candidate	Circle your response.		
Does the mentor candidate truly want to be a mentor?	Yes	No	Unsure
Do they have adequate time to mentor me?	Yes	No	Unsure
Do I like them?	Yes	No	Unsure
Do I respect them?	Yes	No	Unsure
Would I value their advice?	Yes	No	Unsure

Would I be comfortable sharing sensitive information with this person?	Yes	No	Unsure
Can I trust them with sensitive information?	Yes	No	Unsure
Am I confident they will be honest with me?	Yes	No	Unsure
Are our expectations for the relationship well aligned?	Yes	No	Unsure
Am I excited about working with this person?	Yes	No	Unsure
Would I be proud to call them my mentor?	Yes	No	Unsure

Overall impression:

_____

_____

_____

_____

_____

This mentor is a good fit for me. (Circle one.)

Yes   No   Unsure

If yes, we have scheduled an initial meeting for: ___/___/___

Part 3: Observations & Insights
(Complete this section following your initial meeting.)

I learned that…

_____

_____

_____

_____

_____

I will benefit from my mentor in the following ways...

_____

_____

_____

_____

_____

_____

I feel that my mentor is a good fit (or is not a good fit) for me because...

_____

_____

_____

_____

_____

_____

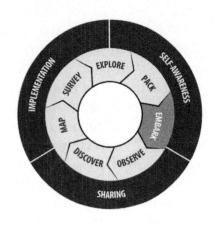

Chapter 12

EMBARK: LAY THE FOUNDATION

"One thing I know; the only ones among you who will be really happy are those who will have sought and found how to serve."
— *Albert Schweitzer*

Getting Started

Once you've selected a date and time for your first meaningful conversation with your mentor, you'll need to decide where and when to meet. Ideally, you will meet in person, but in today's world that might not be realistic. The "right" mentor for you might be miles or even continents away. If distance and time zones are an issue, consider using a technology like Skype to communicate. Although many mentoring partnerships interact primarily by phone or email, there's value in seeing a person real time – even if the connection is virtual.

If you have the opportunity to meet in person, your mentor might suggest a cup of coffee or a neutral place like a local restaurant, in lieu of an office setting. Opt for a venue where you will be most at ease. If an in-office meeting is the most practical locale, then try to find a place that is quiet and welcoming. Look for an out-of-the-way conference room or an office with a view. Try to sit at a small table with comfortable chairs, and avoid a traditional desk at all costs.

Whatever venue you choose, set yourselves up for success. Anticipate and remove any potential distractions or interruptions. Turn off your phones and shut down your computers. Put aside any other work that could divert your attention, and turn your focus to your mentor. Your mentor has reserved time to meet with you, and will expect you to demonstrate an equal level of commitment and focus.

If you'll be meeting in person at a location that's new to you, make sure that you have accurate directions. Plan to arrive at least 15 minutes before your scheduled time. If you're early, use the time to think about what you'd like to learn from your mentor. You might review the questions you plan to ask and reflect on information you'd like to share about yourself.

If you're meeting virtually, test the technology before the meeting to allow yourself time to troubleshoot, if necessary. You may need to download or update software, and you will want to make sure that the technology works well from both sides. You want to get as much time as you can with your mentor, and don't want to waste it trying to figure out how to connect. Your mentor is your host and you are the guest, so do your best to be as gracious and appreciative of their time as you can.

Communicating with Confidence

Sometimes new situations can be anxiety producing, even if you know the outcome will be positive. It's important to manage your body language to exude self-confidence, and demonstrate that you are ready for mentoring and all that comes with it. If you're feeling a bit nervous about engaging with your new mentor, start by taking a few deep breaths. When you calm your thoughts, your body will naturally fall in line. But most importantly, remember that the majority of people who volunteer to mentor are motivated to help others succeed. So, relax.

Think about a time when you met someone new. If you're like most of us, you may have jumped to conclusions about their competency, friendliness, and trustworthiness within seconds. It's human nature to judge others, even when you're trying not to. Sometimes we judge others based on what they say, but often, we reach conclusions from non-verbals. For example, a firm handshake exudes confidence, while a weak one reveals a potential lack of self-assurance. Similarly, direct eye contact says, "I'm comfortable," while averted eyes may indicate trepidation.

We instinctively move in ways that reflect what we are thinking and feeling, and body language goes both ways. First impressions matter, so be aware of what you are communicating directly and indirectly, and pay attention to how your mentor might be feeling as you attempt to establish a foundation for the relationship.

Our communication can be affected by our body language, which often accurately reflects what we are really thinking and feeling. You've probably heard that non-verbal cues account for 55 percent of our overall communication. But of course, it's all subject to interpretation. A single gesture can mean a variety of things depending on the circumstances. Whether you're trying to ensure that your own communication reflects your gratitude for your mentor or whether your goal is to ensure that your mentor is comfortable, here are some tips to keep in mind.

- **Leaning back or leaning in.** It's perfectly natural for self-confident people to lean back in their chairs. However, pay attention when they lean forward. Leaning in could mean that they are engaged in the conversation, and are interested in what you have to say. At the same time, though, note their facial expression and tone of voice. Leaning forward with a furrowed brow suggests confusion or annoyance.

- **Crossed limbs.** Experts agree that uncrossed limbs, legs and arms, show that parties are at ease with each other. However, if your mentor crosses their legs or arms, it could mean that they are feeling defensive or that they disagree with what you're saying. Then, again, crossed legs could simply be a comfortable position for your mentor. Pay attention to what else they are saying – verbally and non-verbally – to determine how they are feeling.

- **Head nodding.** People generally nod their heads in agreement, which can be a good thing if you are hoping to align with your mentor. However, if your mentor's head is bobbing constantly, it may mean that they have lost interest. The more you nod, the more you appear to be tuning out. Be aware of your own movements. Stay in the moment and nod only when you really mean it. If your mentor is nodding frequently, try talking less and asking more questions to capture their attention.

- **Eye contact.** Looking others squarely in the eye is generally a sign of self-confidence. Our eyes tell the truth about our mood, interest, and intentions. Eyes can communicate a lot of information with little observation. For example, frequent blinking can indicate nervousness, while infrequent blinking results from boredom. Darting eyes could signal insecurity, or be a sign that your mentor is looking to escape. (Let's hope the latter is not the case.) If maintaining eye contact is difficult for you, try this: focus on the area of your mentor's face just below their eyes. This will reinforce a friendly, non-threatening relationship.

- **Smiling.** A genuine smile is virtually impossible to fake. While a manufactured smile (like the ones we make when someone taking a photo says, "Cheese") is limited to a disingenuous showing of the teeth, a true smile encompasses one's eyes and cheeks. A fake smile could indicate that someone is uncomfortable or is fudging the truth, while a genuine smile indicates ease and enjoyment.

With all of this in mind, the most important thing to remember is to give your mentor your complete attention at all times. Be fully present. Listen to what they have to say, verbally and non-verbally. If they appear perplexed, ask a question to better understand their reaction. If they look like they have a question, encourage them to ask it. If they appear particularly interested in something you said, ask them to elaborate. Keep in mind that mentorships are often bound by fairly short timelines. If your plan is to work with your mentor for a year, and to meet once a month, you may only see them twelve times. So, make every moment count. The faster you learn how to interpret your mentor's communication cues, the faster you'll get to know them, and the more you will benefit from their advice and counsel.

You should also be conscious of your own body language and the signals you might be sending. Contrived postures, such as a power pose, can work for some, but can appear unnatural for others. So, keep your communication honest and genuine.

When communicating with your mentor remember to:

- Greet your mentor with a firm handshake, a nice smile and a confident greeting.

- Be fully attentive. Put your phone away and focus on the conversation.

- Remove all distractions. Close your laptop, move the flower arrangement from the center of the table, and select a seat that allows you to make a good connection with your mentor.

- Demonstrate your interest by leaning in, asking questions, nodding your head appropriately, agreeing with your mentor, and restating important points.

- Speak clearly, with a confident voice, at just the right volume. Avoid too many "uh-hums," "uhs," and "likes," and watch your language. No matter how comfortable you feel, inappropriate language is always distasteful and will rarely serve you well. Keep it professional.

Sharing Information

The first meeting is the time to get to know your mentor, and to set the ground rules for how you'll work together. Although your mentor may serve more in a leadership role – advising you on what to do next, what to think about, and where to turn for help – the relationship exists to help you meet your professional goals. The onus is on you to make sure your mentor knows as much as possible about you and where you're headed. Make it easy for your mentor to get to know you by telling them everything you think is relevant. Going forward, it will be important for you to be as open and honest with your mentor as you can be. Don't expect them to pry it out of you.

For your first meeting, plan to bring a copy of your résumé for you and your mentor to review together. Tell your mentor which assignments you found most valuable and why, which assignments were the most challenging, which were a waste of time, which led to other opportunities, and anything else about your career that you feel is noteworthy. This will help your mentor get a sense of who you are and will help them begin to see how they might help.

You can also share the results of your Mentee Self-Assessment. It can be a good way to talk about your strengths and developmental opportunities in the context of your career aspirations. You may want to tell your mentor about a newly-acquired skill or discuss recent progress toward overcoming a weakness. Ask your mentor to weigh in on how they feel your strengths and weaknesses might play out as you continue your career ascent. You might find that your weaknesses aren't relevant and that focusing on a single, important strength could differentiate you from others competing for the same position or project.

Bear in mind that, although you may have entered into the mentoring relationship to further your professional development, your personal life is not irrelevant. Unlike a coach who is merely teaching you a skill, a mentor's goal is to provide guidance and to help you find a path that is right for you. To do that, they need to understand how your career goals fit within the broader context of your life.

Talking about your childhood, your family, and your interests can provide context for the decisions that you made along the way. It can help to explain unrealistic fears and unrecognized biases that could become barriers to achieving your goals. It could also point to your motivations for achievement. So, while you're talking about your career history, you might also want to discuss personal successes and challenges that have shaped your personality and preferences. By sharing personal stories, you'll reveal something about you that can't quickly be found on the internet, and you'll likely foster compassion and understanding from others. In fact, you may find that you and your mentor have had similar life experiences, or identify connections that you could leverage.

But don't feel like you have to spill your guts and reveal everything at once. Take it slowly. Make sure your mentor earns your trust before you tell them everything. Always be up front about your weaknesses, and where you think you need the most help at this point in your career. Before you share something that may be uncomfortable, you might want to ask for confirmation that your discussions will remain between the two of you. Maintaining confidences is a critical part of building trust and an important part of mentoring. Asking your mentor for a guarantee of non-disclosure will give them a chance to demonstrate that they are trustworthy, and will give you the opportunity to show that trust and discretion are important to you.

Developing a Plan

During your initial get-together, don't gloss over your career plans. Telling your mentor everything they ever wanted to know about you is great background detail, but the goal is not to dwell in the past, it's to help you take your next steps forward. Focus on where you're headed more than where you've been.

As you are discussing your career goals, keep an open mind. Although you might believe you have a perfect, well-orchestrated plan to get you where you want to go and exactly when you want to get there, your mentor may see your path from a different perspective. To get the most from the mentorship, be open to an alternative approach and perhaps even a different destination.

You may want to start by asking your mentor where it *looks like* you're headed. That is, based on your track record, where might they expect to see you in three to five years? What does your experience so far suggest about where you might land next? Talk about how their insights align with your areas of interest.

Through discussion, your mentor might identify a past position that qualifies you for a whole new area of the business that you hadn't even considered. They may uncover strengths that you didn't know you had or that you didn't think were very important. Your mentor might be aware of an opening that would leapfrog you toward your ultimate dream job faster than your planned route, or they may have heard about a project that can help you obtain the experience you need to be successful in your next position. The best mentors will look at your career path from a strategic and holistic perspective. Your aim should be to give them a lot to think about as they ponder appropriate recommendations.

Once you confirm realistic expectations, work with your mentor to break your overarching objective into individual monthly goals that you can review at each meeting. Breaking larger goals into manageable steps will help you to calendar the tasks that align with your desired destination.

By the end of this meeting, you and your mentor should be in a position to develop a high-level plan with realistic and attainable goals for the duration of the mentorship. Whether you aspire to be promoted, are seeking a lateral move, or are pursuing an entirely new path, your mentor can assist you in breaking your larger goals into manageable steps that will help you arrive at your intended destination.

Setting Ground Rules

Along with a plan, it will be important to implement some guiding principles to ensure a successful and productive relationship. To avoid hurt feelings and misunderstandings, take a proactive approach to establishing rules of behavior that will help you and your mentor feel confident about how the relationship will work. Talk through some dos and don'ts together, and be sure you're treating your mentor the way you would like to be treated. While you and your mentor will want to decide what is realistic and appropriate, consider the following common agreements.

- We both understand that the mentoring relationship is temporary (typically 12 months). Although we may elect to continue the relationship beyond 12 months, we'll broach that subject at the end of this phase of the mentorship.

- We commit to regular meetings. (___ times per week/month/year)

- We agree to start and end each meeting on time.

- We agree to mutually provide open, honest, and tactful feedback.

- We agree to keep all commitments.

- We agree to keep all conversations confidential.

- We agree to work through minor concerns with the knowledge that the mentor wants the best for the mentee.

- We agree to continually evaluate the relationship and look for ways to improve our styles and manner of communication.

- We agree to establish clear responsibilities and to hold each other accountable.

- We agree to honor each other's expertise and experience. (In particular, the mentee agrees to not discount what the mentor brings to the table.)

- We agree to put interruptions aside (cell phones off, computer closed, door shut).

- We agree to make best use of our time together.

You may decide to add more expectations that take into account your industry or work environment. You may choose to delete or modify some because they aren't relevant. Ultimately, the list should be your own. The agreements you jointly establish will help to ensure productive meetings and will help to avoid problems down the line. By broaching the conversation, you'll also demonstrate how invested you are in the relationship and how much you value your mentor's time.

Wrapping up the First Meeting

The typical first meeting will last an hour to an hour-and-a-half, depending on your mentor's schedule and availability. Don't expect more time than that, but be appreciative if you happen to catch your mentor on a day when it's possible to spend more time together. Then again, if you finish up in 45 minutes, don't be disappointed. The meetings and interactions throughout the mentorship may be extended or brief. Mentoring isn't about the amount of time you spend together; it's about the quality of your communication.

Regardless of the duration of the meeting, be sure to conclude the conversation by thanking your mentor for investing in you. At the end of the exchange, your mentor will have a head full of lots of details about your life, your work, and your ambitions. These details will need to be weighed and considered before your mentor can decide where to focus future advice and efforts. Before you leave, review your to-dos and assignments to make sure you captured everything correctly, and confirm the date, time and location for your next meeting.

MENTORING IN ACTION

George Roberts and Paul Zed were waiters at a popular restaurant. Both had waited tables for most of their lives, but neither loved the job. Years before, George had attended culinary school, but ran out of money and had to drop out. He had always planned to go back, but the timing was never right. Paul, on the other hand, had developed quite a reputation as a self-trained baker. He was baking pies in his home kitchen, which he sold to friends and family during the holiday season.

During breaks, George and Paul would spend their time talking about baking and exchanging recipes. They dreamed of opening a bakery in their small, but vibrant town. They brainstormed, researched the market, and prepared a business plan, and acknowledged that their planning was hypothetical and that the chances of them truly opening a bakery were slim. Still, George and Paul shared their dream with anyone who was willing to listen.

Paul's family encouraged them to take a risk. His brother even offered to back the business. As the two continued to talk about the possibilities with others, their dream started to take on a life of its own. But they knew that, even with some financial support, opening and running a bakery wouldn't be easy. George's culinary background would help, and they certainly knew how to delight potential patrons, but Paul worried that his at-home bakery experience wasn't enough to ensure success.

One evening, the two were on a break when the restaurant owner walked in. She said, "Hey, guys. I heard you two are ready to open a bakery." The men were caught off guard, and immediately worried they'd both lose their jobs, but it turned out that the restaurant owner had always thought the town needed a good bakery. In time, she became one of their biggest supporters. In fact, she introduced them to Cameron Bonaire, a well-known pastry chef and owner of a wildly successful patisserie in a nearby metropolitan area.

Like George and Paul, Cameron had transitioned from a restaurant job to a business owner, and he was willing to share his experience and lessons learned. Cameron offered to allow each of them to work in the bakery one day a week for 6 months – George on Wednesdays, the busiest day of the week; and Paul on Sundays, to learn about the "brunch crowd."

During that time, the two soon-to-be business partners learned the business and refined their plans. Cameron confirmed that many of their ideas were good ones, and steered them away from others. In time, the two friends were able to secure a small business loan. With that, and support from friends and family, they opened their first bakery. Now, they own three. They credit much of their success to their mentor, and of course some of their success to their delicious baked goods that keep people waiting in line for hours!

Embark on the Mentoring Journey

Complete this worksheet following the initial meeting with your mentor.

Part 1: The Initial Meeting
My mentor appeared...
(Ex. Interested, distracted, engaged, unemotional, frustrated, committed, etc.)

_____

_____

We talked about...

_____

_____

_____

I learned that my mentor...

_____

_____

_____

Rules for the mentorship...

_____

_____

_____

_____

_____

_____

Part 2: Goals for Mentoring

We agreed to work together for _____ months from __/__/__ to __/__/__.

My Overarching Objective is...

_____

_____

Monthly Goals		
Month	Goal	Scheduled Meetings

Comments:

_____

_____

_____

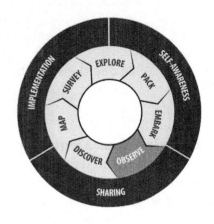

Chapter 13

OBSERVE: TUNE IN

"Better than a thousand days of diligent study is one day with a great teacher."
—*Japanese Proverb*

As you meet with your mentor, you'll discuss your progress and talk about how to handle stumbling blocks along the way. Your mentor will listen, share their observations and insights, and offer you the opportunity to benefit from their experience. Don't expect your mentor to lead the discussion.

To get the most from your interactions, do your homework. Take time before each session to reflect on your progress. Consider the questions below:

- Which assigned tasks did I complete? What did I learn from the exercise?

- Which assignments proved more challenging than I had anticipated? Why?

- What new tasks do I think I need to tackle in order to move forward?

- How am I feeling about what I've accomplished?

- What questions do I have for my mentor?

Bringing Your Mentor up to Speed

An experienced mentor will listen to your progress report, and will almost always follow up with a ton of questions. Rest assured, their intent is not to interrogate you or to question your actions. Instead, they will use inquiry to learn more about you, and to help to determine how to offer the "right" advice.

You can prepare by anticipating the questions they might ask. Many of their questions will undoubtedly relate directly to your assigned to-dos, while others may be more general. Don't be thrown off. Remember that your mentor is advising you in the context of your life and your previous experiences. So, answer the questions openly and honestly and let your mentor do the rest of the work.

Looking Back to Move Forward

While you can't anticipate every question your mentor will ask, you can certainly think through how you would answer some of the more typical questions. To get you started, we've developed a list of frequently asked questions, and have categorized them by topic. To prepare for your discussions, you can start with the first topic and work your way through the list, or you can begin with the area that interests you most.

Take time to write as much as you can about each topic. Sometimes, the most important information is buried a bit below surface. You may want to capture some initial thoughts, then set your work aside and revisit it later. You might find that time between working sessions could give your mind the break it needs to recall valuable experiences that could play a role in your future success.

If you'd like to work through all of the questions in a single sitting, you certainly can. But we'd recommend setting aside some time for each topic. It might take a few days, or even a few weeks to make your way through the list. You've likely already had a robust adventure-filled life complete with ups and downs, accomplishments and failures.

You have no doubt developed a unique perspective on the world that has resulted in your own set of values, biases and core beliefs. So, don't rush the playback. Allow yourself ample time to think and respond.

Growing up. Many of our most powerful beliefs and preferences are formed during childhood. These beliefs may be empowering or limiting. Either way, they can affect our behaviors and our choices. Reflect on your childhood experiences, your family's attitudes about success, and your early role models. Consider how others have impacted your career choices as you answer the questions below.

- Where did you grow up? How did your hometown influence you later in life?

- How did your parents make a living?

- Did you have siblings? If so, what were they like? How did they influence you?

- Were there people in your youth who affected your career choices?

- What are your most vivid memories about growing up? Are they happy or not so happy?

- Where did you go to school?

- What do you remember about your experiences in the classroom?

- Did you get good grades?

- What were your favorite subjects? Why?

- What were your least favorite subjects? Why?

- Where did you excel? (Were you strong in sports, the arts or some other extracurricular activity?)

- Did you have a favorite teacher?

- Who were your best friends? How would you describe them?

- Did you go to college? If so, where?

- What was your major?

- What did you like most about college?

Attitude is everything. Your beliefs about what you are capable of accomplishing can create endless possibilities or can prevent you from taking any action at all. If you are wildly optimistic, you might pursue opportunities that others don't think are possible. However, if your beliefs are self-limiting you might give up before you try. What beliefs do you hold that may have affected your path and your decisions? How have assumptions impacted your choices in life?

- Why did you choose the college you attended?

- How did you pick your major? What influenced your decision?

- How did you choose your career? Are you happy with your decision?

- Why did you accept your current position? Did you have other offers? If so, how did you make a decision?

- What would you like to do next? Why aren't you in *that* position now? What is holding you back?

- What is your ultimate career goal?

- What do you think you'll need to do to achieve your goal?

- What strengths will help you accomplish your goal? What weaknesses might stand in your way?

- Who within your organization can help you achieve your goal?

- What would you do if nothing stood in your way? What is standing in your way?

- What do other people recognize as your strengths? How does that make you feel?

Your job history. Examining your career history can reveal a lot about your priorities, goals and preferences. Think about your career track and be ready to share with your mentor.

- What was your first job?

- Why do you think you were offered your first job over other equally talented candidates?

- What other notable positions have you held?

- What skills and abilities have helped you to be successful in each position?

- What didn't you like about each position you've held?

- Did you have to overcome any weaknesses as you progressed in your career? How did you do it?

- Why did you decide to leave each position in your career history?

- What was appealing about your next job that made it more interesting than your last?

- What was your favorite job? Why?

- What was your least favorite job? Why?

- How did you land at your current employer or in your current position?

- How do you feel about the work you are currently doing? What would make it more satisfying?

- Describe the perfect job. How is it different from the job you hold now?

Ghosts of bosses past. Good bosses can open doors that might otherwise have been closed, while bad bosses can get in the way of career progress. Your mentor might benefit from learning about the managers who helped you along the way, as well as those who may have hindered your progress or caused you to doubt your abilities. A mentor can help you analyze previous working relationships and identify the characteristics you might look for in a future boss. Often, the manager you choose to work for is as important as the job you choose to accept. A mentor can be objective in determining whether the position *and* the reporting structure will be a good fit. Answers to the following questions could provide insights to help your mentor help you.

- Who was your best boss? Why?

- Were your personalities similar or different?

- What did this person make possible for you?

- Did this boss provide training or guidance? In what way?

- What kind of feedback did your boss provide? What types of observations and advice did you find most helpful?

- Which of this individual's characteristics or strengths did/do you try to emulate?

- Did your "best" boss help you network with others in the company?

- Who was your worst boss?

- How was this person different from your best boss?

- What could this boss have done differently to be a more positive influence on you?

- Did this individual affect how you approached certain projects? In what way?

- What kind of feedback have you received consistently from managers or supervisors?

- Do you agree or disagree with their advice? Did you act on it?

Past assignments. Regardless of your title, most jobs involve enjoyable and not-so-enjoyable responsibilities. Think about what you liked and didn't like about each of your past positions, and reflect on how you handled the parts of each job that you didn't enjoy. The same is true for projects and special assignments. Which tasks played to your strengths? How did you approach more challenging elements of the work?

- What were your roles and responsibilities in each of your past jobs?

- Did your positions vary widely in terms of roles and responsibilities?

- Have you ever been asked to take on responsibilities above and beyond those listed in your job description? Why or why not?

- How did you approach the tasks that were challenging for you or that you didn't enjoy?

- Did you ever turn down a request to tackle a specific project or task? If so, why? Did that affect others' perceptions of you?

- Have you ever declined a project or job because you didn't think you were qualified? What was the position? What skills or abilities did you believe you were lacking?

- Did you ever apply for an assignment or a job that you didn't get?

- What strengths have helped you to be successful in your career?

- Are there specific skills you lack that you believe could have helped you in past jobs?

How your manager sees you. With some exceptions, performance appraisals and job reviews can be nerve-wracking, especially when you're not sure what to expect. Think back to the reviews you have experienced in your career; what did you learn from them?

- How would you describe the performance appraisals you've received?

- Have you generally agreed with the feedback you've received? Was there a time when you didn't agree?

- What strengths regularly surface as contributors to your success?

- What areas have been identified for improvement?

- Have you generally taken your managers' advice? Why or why not?

- During which assignment or job did you receive your best performance review(s)? Why was the review deserved?

- During which assignment did you receive your worst performance review(s)? What could you have done differently to improve your performance and/or your evaluation?

- How would you summarize your current performance?

When you failed. It may take several months before you reach the topic of failures. In fact, you might never have the chance to talk about some of these areas. But reflecting on the potholes in your career path to date can only help you and your mentor move further and faster toward your goals. Although you might not want to revisit experiences where you weren't as successful as you might have hoped, sharing what went wrong can be a big help to a mentor in search of ways to offer you guidance. They might be able to spot bad habits or tendencies that could be easily corrected, and they may be able to help you anticipate situations that could interfere with your progress or threaten your success. Take a few moments for introspection by responding to the following questions:

- Has there ever been a project or assignment in which you did not achieve the results you wanted or expected? Why did you struggle?

- Did your disappointment amount to a misstep or result in a failed project or effort?

- How much of the "failure" was your fault? How much of the blame would you place on others who may have let you down?

- Were you ever involved in a failed project or effort that was completely your fault? If so, how did you handle the disappointment?

- Could you have done anything to avoid the failure or misstep?

- What have you learned from past failures?

- What types of projects do you think you might struggle with today?

- Is there anything you can do to prevent that?

- Sometimes, we avoid failure or disappointment by playing it safe. Have you ever turned down or missed an opportunity because you were afraid to fail?

Your beliefs about success. Just as evaluating past failures can be a useful and informative exercise, so can a discussion about your successes and how you achieved them. Think back to a time when you ran a successful project, led a team to victory, or exceeded the expectations for a job or position. To what do you attribute your accomplishments? Use the following prompts to reflect on your successes.

- Describe a recent successful assignment.

- What made it/you successful?

- Would others consider the assignment a success? Why or why not?

- Did anyone else contribute in a significant way? If so, how?

- If you had to do it all over again, is there anything you would do differently?

- What challenges did you have to overcome?

- What did you learn from the experience that will help you in the future?

Your champions. If you've been rising in the ranks at your current employer, or if you have risen in the past, you likely have people around you who are cheering you on. How would you describe your greatest supporters? Who has advocated on your behalf?

- Describe the individuals who have helped you get to where you are today.

- Do you have any role models?

- Would you consider your manager or supervisor one of your fans?

- How have past managers or supervisors helped your career?

- If you had to request three letters of recommendation, to whom would you turn?

- Do you have advocates in other companies?

- Are you well known through a professional organization, association or trade group?

- Do you volunteer for any causes or charities? Are you actively involved?

- Who would you like to meet that you don't already know?

A solutions orientation. They say that some people are natural problem-solvers, coming up with solutions almost instinctively. Others prefer to examine a variety of approaches to a challenge before landing on a course of action. Which camp would you say you're in? (Note: There is no right or wrong answer here.)

- When given an assignment, do you prefer to follow the instructions to the letter, or vary your approach when you believe there is an opportunity for improvement?

- Are there certain situations when you believe it's important to follow instructions exactly as you are told?

- Was there ever a time when you were asked to follow instructions, but didn't? How did it turn out?

- How do you tend to approach unexpected situations or problems?

- How often do you turn to others for advice? Does it usually help?

- What other resources do you rely on for inspiration and guidance?

- What do you do when you've struggled to solve a problem, but can't find a solution?

Use Active Listening Skills

While your mentor is asking questions to learn more about you, you'll likely spend a lot more time talking than listening. Although it might be tempting to tell your mentor about everything you've done, seen or experienced, you'll derive the greatest benefit from listening to their stories and advice. So, even if you're asked to tell your life story, remember to allow ample opportunity for valuable feedback from your mentor. During your initial conversations, it's okay to aim for a ratio of 75% (you talking) to 25% (them talking). But by about the third meeting, your conversations should become more balanced, 50% (you talking), 50% (them talking).

As you share information with your mentor, pay close attention to the follow-up questions they ask, and the comments they make. Your mentor might notice something that you never have. For example, they might see a minor change in your facial expressions that could reveal your *true* feelings about a past experience. Or they may note a change in your voice pattern when describing your volunteer work that could hint at your true calling.

When your mentor is speaking, make sure they know that you are actively listening to their observations and insights.

- Meet in a quiet space to reduce or eliminate most distractions. Stay focused on what your mentor is telling you.

- Confirm that you heard what they said by nodding your head or reiterating a key point.

- Ask a follow-up question to better understand the point your mentor is trying to make, or to learn more about their history and experiences.

- Smile and use facial expressions to acknowledge that you heard what has been said.

- Check your body language to be sure you're encouraging information sharing (uncross your arms, maintain eye contact, leaning in, etc.).

- Summarize what you heard and add to a thought or recommendation.

Seeking Support

While asking questions might be an important way for your mentor to engage with you, they will also bring value to the relationship by offering information and resources. Although your mentor is not required to connect you with other people in their network or to point you in the direction of resources that could help, they might be willing to do so, if asked. They may also be aware of educational opportunities that could aid in your development or help to expand your knowledge in an area of relevance. Resources might include:

- **People.** People who can help may work within, or outside, your organization. They may hold, or may have held, the position to which you aspire, or may be able to provide appropriate guidance given your goals and aspirations.

- **Organizations.** You might also find help, encouragement, and inspiration by connecting with an organization with expertise in your area of interest. These organizations can include professional groups, clubs, trade or civic associations, as well as other local and/or volunteer groups.

- **Training and education.** Training programs and educational opportunities can help you develop skills and abilities related to topics such as: public speaking, people management, conflict resolution or others. Today, there are so many options available to enhance your knowledge and skills that you might find it difficult to determine which option is best for you. Your mentor may have experience with an institution, may be knowledgeable about a course, and may be in a position to weigh in as you consider your alternatives.

- **Coaches.** Coaches and mentors are both valuable. But they are different. Mentors generally focus on longer-term, more strategic issues related to life and career. Coaches can help you learn a specific skill or develop a needed capability. Sometimes, a one-on-one coach can be useful for tackling a specific issue or skill such as branding, personal image, on-camera interviews, finance, etc. Lean on your mentor to help you determine if, and when, engaging a professional coach could be helpful.

- **Books and publications, blogs, videos and websites.** Whether you are looking for inspiration, education or advice, there's a respected guru in almost every area that you could imagine. It's highly likely that your mentor can point you in the right direction.

Writing It Down

Don't be surprised if your mentor takes notes in a journal to remind them of your discussions from week-to-week or month-to-month. Your mentor might document important milestones, track goals you set, and record insights and recommendations they shared with you. They will probably also keep a record of your to-dos, as well as their own commitments and action items. Recording what they hear will help them recall your discussions at a later date. In our experience, good mentors commit to your ongoing success. A completed journal will serve as a track record of your joint progress over time.

For many of the same reasons, you should invest in your own journal. First of all, it's just plain smart to take notes about the information you share and the advice and counsel your mentor provides. Having all your mentoring notes in one place is both efficient and effective. By consolidating your notes, you avoid having to keep track of tiny slips of paper and random sticky notes, and you ensure that you and your mentor will always be on the same page. Secondly, what may seem unimportant during one session may become pivotal later in the process. Recording your discussions prevents you from forgetting critical details. Finally, if you capture notes from your meetings, list your questions, record your thoughts and feelings between interactions with your mentor, log your assignments, and include key learnings, by the end of the mentorship you'll have a detailed record of your progress and a reminder of your successes and challenges.

One of the biggest benefits of a journal is that it forces you to put pen to paper. Studies have shown that the mere act of writing something down significantly increases your chances of achieving it. So, take the time to write it down. Start by describing what you hope to accomplish and how you plan to reach your goals with help from your mentor. Then, include as many details about your conversations and thoughts as possible. In time, you and your mentor may identify patterns and trends that could inform their advice as well as potential next steps to advance your career.

MENTORING IN ACTION

April Cast earned her MBA in marketing, and went on to work for a division of a major corporation. She was quickly promoted, and began to see herself as a future executive, despite the fact that she had never really been interested in the corporate world. April was on track, working her way through the leadership ranks, when she was approached by Anderson Whaite, the Senior Vice President of the business unit.

Anderson offered her a position as a business analyst, working directly for him. Although April wasn't crazy about the job description, she was flattered that he asked, and saw the move as another step up the corporate ladder. She happily accepted. The position tested her business and analytical skills, and she grew in ways she hadn't expected. Anderson treated her as much as a peer as he did a direct report, and for that she was thankful.

As a business analyst, April was responsible for gathering, analyzing and reporting information that helped Anderson and other leaders run the business. It often required the team to work closely as they pored over data, so they got to know each other pretty well. During one late evening at the office, the group started talking about things they do in their spare time. (Laughing that they had very little time to spare.) April's colleagues revealed a variety of interests. One person spent his spare time as a semi-professional fly fisherman. Another shared that he bought and renovated vacation rentals. And yet another talked about her passion for horse racing.

Anderson was next in line to talk about his interests. He said that in his spare time he was writing a book, and that he had written several pieces of fiction under a pen name. He said, "It's something I've done since I was in my 20's. Not many people know about it, but it keeps me sane." All at once, the air went out of the room, as his team gasped in surprise. "How in the world?" someone asked. "As you know, I'm a pretty planful guy," he replied. And everyone laughed.

April was humbled by their incredible personal lives, and reflected on the fact that she didn't have much of a life outside of work. When it was her turn, she quickly changed the subject and reminded the group that they'd better get back to work, if they hoped to get home before sunrise.

The next day, April popped in to Anderson's office. She told him that she had always wanted to write a book, but could never seem to find the time. Then, she said, "But if you're the SVP, and you can do it, what's my excuse?" He asked her to have a seat, and they talked for about an hour.

April shared that she wanted to publish a how-to book, and wondered how he was able to write and work at the same time. Over the next 12 months, Anderson reserved time to help April plan and craft her first publication. He also found time to coach her through the process of getting her book sold. Although she ultimately self-published, she is forever thankful for his mentoring.

April eventually left her corporate job to focus entirely on writing and speaking. Anderson has since retired, but the two keep in touch. He often reviews her books and is her best and most trusted critic. April is now a full-time author and popular speaker, thanks – in part – to the mentor who helped her live her true passion.

OBSERVATION GUIDE

Use Part 1 of this guide to plan your discussion, and Part 2 to record observations and recommendations from the meeting.

Part 1: Reflections

By reviewing the topics in this chapter I learned that...

_____

_____

_____

_____

_____

I'd like to share information about...

_____

_____

_____

_____

_____

I'd like to ask about the following resources:

_____

_____

_____

_____

_____

Part 2: Insights & Observations

My mentor's initial observations:

_____

_____

_____

_____

_____

My mentor's initial recommendations and resources:

_____

_____

_____

_____

_____

Topics to discuss during the next meeting:

_____

_____

_____

_____

_____

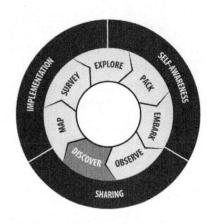

Chapter 14

DISCOVER: FEEDBACK AND ADVICE

"Few things in the world are more powerful than a positive push.
A smile. A word of optimism and hope.
A 'you can do it' when things are tough."
—Richard M. De Vos

Getting Feedback

After sharing your plans, dreams and aspirations with your mentor, it's time for a reality check. By now, your mentor should have insight into your past, a good sense of where you're headed, and a clear understanding of what you hope to accomplish. With that information in hand, it's time for your mentor to dive in and give you some feedback.

Perhaps your mentor has been offering suggestions all along, but the early stages of mentoring are really about looking for patterns and trends, identifying strengths and potential weaknesses, and searching for a path that is the best path for you. Where *should* you be headed? Are your professional goals truly in line with the lifestyle you desire? Does your target position encompass responsibilities that will bring you joy, or might you benefit from a subtle – or not-so-subtle –change in direction?

Are you nervous about hearing your mentor's observations and insights? Most mentees are, at least initially. Keep in mind, your mentor isn't in the relationship to rip you apart or tear you down. Their goal is to make sure you have all the support you need to achieve your goals. The feedback and advice you're about to receive is intended to get you on the right path, or to confirm you're already there, and to help to accelerate your development. There's nothing to be worried about. You must know and trust that your mentor is in the relationship to help you succeed, and that all of their feedback comes from a good place.

Observations and Insights

Expect to hear more positive than negative comments up front, as your mentor summarizes your career progress. Their praise is warranted, as few mentors would agree to counsel you if you weren't a high-performing employee or person on the rise. Enjoy the accolades, but realize that there's value in learning what you need to work on, so pay attention to what comes next. Listen to the way in which your mentor characterizes your career, your reputation and goals. Is their portrayal accurate? Do you think they really "get" where you are coming from? Do they seem to understand where you are headed? Do you think they believe you can achieve your short- and long-term goals?

Odds are you'll agree with many of your mentor's insights and recommendations, but you may not agree with all of them. In fact, some observations and comments may sting a bit. Be ready to hear things you might not like or that you might not want to hear. If your mentor had nothing but positive things to say, how would you improve?

Mentors offer constructive criticism and advice because they want to help you move to the next level of your career, and they want to make sure you're prepared when you get there. If they didn't care, they would gloss over your weaknesses, pretending not to have seen them. But since you know they're there, you should not be surprised, nor hurt, when they are brought to your attention. Be brave. Be strong. No one is perfect. In fact, you should cherish the candid feedback. Few people in your life will have the courage to tell you the truth. Hearing what you suspect about yourself should simply confirm that your mentor has spent a fair amount of time truly getting to know you. The real work begins when you combine your efforts to move forward.

As you start to take in your mentor's words of wisdom, pay attention to the language they use. If you feel their descriptions are off base, gently correct your mentor's impressions. Don't become argumentative; instead, ask if you can clarify a point you may have previously misstated. Suggesting the misunderstanding was your fault is common courtesy, and will be appreciated by your mentor.

But don't correct too soon. With a bit of introspection, you might find that your mentor's observations are actually spot on. When someone uncovers a potential blind spot that may be standing in the way of your advancement, they might be dealing a tough blow, but more importantly, they are giving you a priceless gift.

A mentee once told us about a life-changing revelation that she had when working with one of her mentors. The mentee worked for a Fortune 500 company and was quickly climbing the corporate ladder. Her mentor was an Executive Vice President for the same organization. The mentee was in a management position and well on her way to being a senior leader in her own right. As others were becoming aware of her skills and potential, she was being asked more frequently to participate in important discussions, and to weigh in on critical decisions. That meant more meetings with people of influence. The mentee was pleased that others appreciated her input, and she recognized the value of the opportunities she was being given. However, one day, her mentor stopped her in her tracks. She said, "Hey, I need to tell you something. You will never win at a game of poker, or negotiate your position effectively, if you don't get your facial expressions under control." The mentee was taken aback.

The mentor went on to explain that she had noticed that every time an executive made a remark the mentee didn't agree with, the mentee would raise her eyebrows and wrinkle her forehead. In fact, the mentee's nonverbals were so prominent that everyone in the room noticed. The mentor then explained that the mentee's body language often put others on the defensive and created obvious tension in the room.

Although the critical feedback was hard to swallow, the mentee told us that she truly valued her mentor's opinion, so she listened and didn't push back. Instead, she worked to relax her facial muscles during meetings, and was ultimately able to keep her eyebrows in check.

One mentor told a story about the day his mentee asked to spend some time prepping for an upcoming interview. He said that, although it was difficult, he had to let his mentee know that his chances of getting the job he was hoping for were slim...not because he wasn't qualified, but because he had a reputation of being difficult to work with. The truth was that it didn't matter how much time the mentor and his mentee spent talking about how to respond to the interview questions; if the mentee couldn't overcome the perception that he was challenging to work with, he would never be offered the position. At first, the mentee pushed back, but then he acknowledged that his passion could sometimes be confused with confrontation. The mentee initially considered backing out of the interview. But in the end he really wanted the job and knew he was qualified, so he chose to address the issue head-on, and ultimately, he got the job.

Good Advice and Practical Steps

A good mentor will tailor their feedback to help you develop. Most will suggest specific steps you can take to make progress toward your career goals. Although every mentoring relationship is different, your mentor might recommend:

- Joining a specific professional or trade organization for increased visibility and networking

- Registering for a course to help build or further improve a specific skill, such as public speaking or managing people

- Pursuing a larger role on a current project to gain experience or demonstrate your capability

- Exploring job opportunities outside the company or country to gain experience that can be brought back later and position you for a larger role

- Taking advantage of the company's education allowance to earn an advanced degree or certificate

- Becoming more familiar with a technology that is important to the company and could differentiate you from other potential candidates

- Agreeing to mentor a more junior employee to demonstrate your leadership skills and show your commitment to talent development

- Improving business skills like time management, project management or business writing

- Studying the teachings of a recognized author or consultant who may be working with your employer

- Gaining media exposure through article submissions or expert interviews

Even if you are among the very top employees in your organization, there is always something else you can do to enhance your reputation, increase your visibility, or expand your network. Think of your mentor's list of specific steps as a starting point for your personal development, or refer to the list above and add some of your own ideas.

Listen Closely for Tips

Some mentors are direct when sharing their insights; they provide clear and candid feedback and there is absolutely no need to read between the lines. Others may be less comfortable being so direct. If your mentor showers you with praise, but has trouble delivering bad news, you should listen closely to uncover their true impressions. Some mentors will sandwich their real advice between positive statements to soften the blow. But doing so may make it tough to spot the things you really need to work on.

The sandwich technique is a common way to provide feedback. You offer two compliments, and position the improvement opportunity between them. Here's an example: "Your self-confidence and independence have served you well and have earned the respect of your peers and bosses, even though you come across as abrasive at times.

Regardless, I'm sure you'll continue to receive positive performance reviews because you know how to get things done." Did you catch the bad news? Yes, you're abrasive. That's not exactly what anyone wants to hear, but addressing the perception could be the most important thing you could do to advance your career. You don't want to miss critical insights, so listen closely to the transitions. The most important stuff might just follow words like:

- But

- However

- Despite

- Although

- Nevertheless

These lead-ins will generally be followed by potential improvement opportunities, including patterns your mentor has noticed or issues that others may have brought to their attention. Remember that when it comes to feedback from your mentor, "bad" news is never really bad. You can't make a change if you don't know what to work on, and blind spots aren't helpful. So, let your mentor know that you welcome the feedback, and then listen closely.

Your mentor is offering you the benefit of their expertise and experience, so try your best not to become angry or defensive. It's a mentor's job to help you see yourself in a new light, so you can continue to climb the career ladder successfully. Even if you don't agree with their observations and insights at first, ask for more information to try to understand their perspective. But when you ask, ask as you would ask a friend, without any hint of disappointment or frustration.

Some things to watch for as you delve into touchy subjects:

- **Your emotions.** Regardless of how you feel about the feedback, try to keep your outward expression in check. There isn't a mentor on the planet who wants to make you sad or angry. They simply want to help you be your best. They want to help you find ways to leverage your strengths and overcome your weaknesses. So, accept their input in the spirit in which it's offered, with respect and admiration. (If you feel the need to scream, shout or cry, do it in your car after you leave the meeting.)

- **Your tone, pitch, volume and pace.** When we speak, our voices often say more than the words we use. For example, the tone of your voice will tell others whether you are happy, anxious, annoyed, or sad. If you appear irritated your mentor might just shut down, feeling that you aren't ready to hear the truth. This could lead them to question your commitment and your maturity, and could make them wonder whether you are truly ready to benefit from mentoring. So, try to keep your conversations calm and casual, not tense or angry. Likewise, a high-pitched voice could indicate excitement, panic or a lack of control. So, it's wise to use the lower-end of your voice range when you want to appear competent and confident. Volume and pace can also give you away if you are feeling tense. Be aware if your tendency is to raise or lower your voice in stressful situations, or if you have a habit of speaking quickly when you're nervous.

- **Your facial expressions.** Do your best not to scowl or sulk, even if the information you're hearing isn't what you hoped for. Likewise, raised eyebrows or a wide-eyed look of surprise can be disconcerting to a mentor who is simply trying to help. In fact, even your lips can betray your emotions. Pursing your lips can show disagreement, pouting can indicate disappointment or displeasure, and biting your lips can mean that you are nervous. To control your facial expression, try to relax, focus on active listening, breathe, and do your best to control your natural reactions.

- **Your body language.** As we said before, your body language can say just as much as the words you use. Your mentor is here to help you, so try not to close yourself off to their aid. The more you remain calm and focused, the more you'll gain from the discussion. If you shut down, you'll shut down your mentor. So keep your wits about you when you reach the heart of the discussion. Listen. Ask questions. And prepare to act on your mentor's recommendations.

Recognizing Observations and Insights

As you're listening to your mentor's feedback, try to differentiate between what your mentor has seen firsthand (their observations) and how your actions and behaviors might positively or negatively impact your success (their insights). The distinction is important. When offering observations about you and your career, your mentor might refer to your:

- Behavior

- Reactions to situations

- Treatment of others

- Work performance

- Time management

- Ambition

- Strengths

- Weaknesses

- Wardrobe

- Grooming

- Personal hygiene

- Temperament

For example, your mentor might have observed that you tend to leave important tasks to the last minute. This conclusion creates an opportunity to talk about time management and prioritization, which may be weaknesses for you, but strengths for your mentor. It also creates the opportunity to talk about how your strengths and weaknesses might affect your ability to achieve your goals. If procrastination is an issue for you, you could learn from your mentor by asking questions and then heeding their advice. You could ask:

- Was procrastination ever a problem for you?

- How do you make sure that everything gets done?

- Are some things more important to you than others?

If your mentor observes that your image is being negatively impacted by your choice of attire, find out what they believe you should change. Get specific.

- Do you need an expensive new suit right away, or would swapping your sandals for closed-toe shoes be adequate in the short-term?

- Is the issue truly about your style staples, or is it more about how you pull yourself together?

Insights describe the effect that an observed behavior might have on one's ability to succeed. When delivering feedback, it's natural to offer an observation followed by some insight regarding why a change may be needed. Pay close attention when your mentor shares observations and insights because you may concur with the characterization of your behavior, but not realize the impact your actions may be having on your career. For example, your mentor might have observed that you appear extremely comfortable in the midst of senior management, and you might agree. However, while you think your confidence with leadership is a strength, your mentor's insight may reveal that your casual approach is viewed as a lack of respect by some executives. The observation: "You seem completely comfortable with senior management." The insight: "You might not realize that your confidence may be off-putting to some executives." Make sure you don't listen to the observation, yet ignore the insight. Both can be critical for your future.

Your mentor may offer their initial observations and insights during a single session, or they may choose to present them over time. Either way, it's important to truly listen and act on your mentor's advice, since that's where true change can begin to occur. Together you will figure out how to best address your weaknesses and continue to build on your strengths. So, get the tough discussions out of the way, swallow your medicine, and move forward.

During your conversations with your mentor, you will likely receive many compliments. Your mentor can help you turn your strengths into true assets as you climb the career ladder. You might also receive constructive feedback regarding limiting beliefs or behaviors, knowledge gaps, and developmental opportunities. It can be a lot to process, and even a bit confusing. So, don't make assumptions or jump to conclusions. Instead, take time to restate what you heard. Say, "I'd like to repeat what I think you just said to be sure I understood you correctly." And practice summarizing the conversation at the end of each meeting. By cultivating these habits, you'll ensure clarity and understanding.

Where Are We?

Whether the feedback you've received has been largely positive, largely constructive, or evenly balanced, spending a lot of time on introspection can be taxing. After a few potentially emotionally draining discussions, it will be important to stop and take stock of your relationship with your mentor. How do you feel about what you heard? How was it expressed? If your mentor has done a good job, you should be feeling grateful and respected, despite the fact that you might not like everything you've heard.

If, on the other hand, you're feeling attacked or insulted, ask yourself: "Why?" Were you taken off guard by some unexpected comments? Try to separate the content of the discussion from the person who shared the insights. Did your mentor offer their observations and insights with positive intent? If you take an honest look at yourself, could your mentor's feedback be on target? Do you value your mentor's opinions and advice, even though the conversation may have been difficult? Do you want to continue with the relationship?

Sometimes, our greatest growth comes from interacting with people who were willing to offer us candid, constructive feedback and powerful insights. To be sure, mentoring is not for the faint of heart, but it is perfect for those who are up for a challenge and are committed to personal and professional growth. Climbing a ladder of any sort requires thick skin and fortitude. Look inside yourself and find the strength you need to embrace your strengths and recognize your flaws. Any action that you take – no matter how small – will ultimately help you to become a better person.

As each session comes to a close, take time to thank your mentor. Tell them that you appreciate the compliments, as they will keep you motivated and on course. And as difficult as it may have been to hear negative feedback, recognize that sharing difficult news isn't always easy. Make sure your mentor knows how much you appreciate their candor. Finally, remember to express your sincere appreciation for their commitment to helping you achieve your goals, and always confirm the date and time for your next meeting.

Between meetings, take time to digest the feedback. Let it sink in. Think about how a change could positively impact your career and your life. Then, focus on your next steps, and take action.

MENTORING IN ACTION

From the time Marcus was a young child, he always knew that he would grow up to be a lawyer. His father was a lawyer, his grandfather was a lawyer, and so were both of his older sisters. After graduation, Marcus applied and was accepted to one of the most prestigious law schools in the country. He returned home to enjoy the summer before moving on, predictably, toward his destiny.

During his first week back, Marcus connected with some of his high school friends. One of them was working on his dad's political campaign. Marcus thought it would be fun to help out, so he joined a few of his friends, and canvassed the precinct for the candidate. It was even more fun than he had imagined. He spent much of the summer answering phones, writing newsletters, and campaigning.

In the fall, Marcus headed to law school, as planned. And his friend was elected to the City Council. The two kept in touch throughout the year, and the Councilman kept Marcus informed about local politics. The following summer, Marcus returned home, again. He and the Councilman met for lunch. They had been chatting for about an hour, when the Councilman asked, "What do you want to do with your life?"

Marcus was taken aback. No one had ever asked what he wanted to do. After all, he was born to practice law. But somewhere inside, he knew that he was not destined to spend his life trying cases in a courthouse. In fact, in the year he'd been at school, he realized he actually hated law.

Lunch with the Councilman ran into dinner, while the two talked about a career in politics. The Councilman said, "If you're really interested in working in the public sector, a law degree might help, but there's no college major that can prepare you to become a politician. You have to get experience."

Marcus went on to earn his degree, but under the guidance of his mentor he also spent time volunteering in the public sector. He worked on numerous campaigns, ran for local offices, and perfected the skills that would help him on the campaign trail. He has since served on several successful national campaigns and hopes to run for the United States Senate.

Although his mentor has moved on from the local to the national level, his closest friends continue to call him "The Councilman." Marcus said, "The Councilman gave me the greatest gift anyone could ask for. He stopped me in my tracks, and helped me see that life is best when you pursue the thing that makes you happy, even if it's not the thing that others expected you to do. I am forever grateful."

Discovery Tool

Use this tool to capture your mentor's feedback and plan next steps.

Part 1: Observations and Insights

Observations from prior meetings:

_____

_____

_____

_____

_____

Insights from prior meetings:

_____

_____

_____

_____

_____

Based on these insights and observations, I plan to:

_____

_____

_____

_____

_____

Topics to discuss during the next meeting:

_____

_____

_____

_____

_____

_____

_____

_____

_____

_____

_____

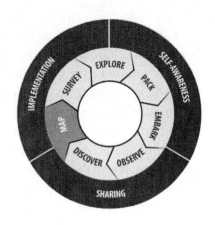

Chapter 15

MAP: GOAL-SETTING

"Confidence, like art, never comes from having all the answers; it comes from being open to all the questions."
—Earl Gray Stevens

Mentoring relationships exist because individuals, like you, want and need guidance and advice from people who have been where you want to go, or who are now in the position you are striving for. Often, those who have succeeded in achieving their own career goals are happy to share their learnings with others with the potential to follow in their footsteps.

But the relationship between a mentor and a mentee is ultimately defined by the mentee's unique goals and objectives. Without some sense of what you want to achieve and idea of where you might need help, it will be difficult for a mentor to assess how they can help you hit your target.

All mentees have different goals. Your goal may be to earn a long overdue promotion. Or it might be to find a more challenging job with a new employer. You might want to negotiate a move or a work-from-home position. Or you might want to transition from a for-profit position to a leadership role at a not-for-profit. When drafting your goals, begin with your top priorities in mind.

Although most formal mentoring programs last about 12 months, less formal relationships may ebb and flow as you need help, and fade away as you make progress on your own. Once you've had a few meetings, you should start to get a sense of each other's personalities, quirks, preferences and pet peeves. And you should come to a point when the shared goals for your mentorship become almost obvious. Regardless of the anticipated duration of your relationship, it's important to agree on your goals and desired outcomes as a way of tracking your progress. Without stated goals and clearly defined targets, it will be difficult for either you or your mentor to evaluate your progress.

Your Long- and Short-Term Goals

Although your immediate focus may be on your current job, or your next job, it's also important to take time to talk with your mentor about your long-term career goals. Planning for 10 or even 20 years from now is very different from planning for where you want to be in 6-12 months. In a year, you may aspire to earn a promotion or complete an important assignment successfully, but in 10 or 20 years you may want to be running your own business or leading an organization. To reach your ultimate goal, you will likely need to develop skills very different from the ones you'll use to win that next promotion.

To begin a discussion with you mentor about your future plans and long-term aspirations, you might want to:

- Share your ultimate career goal. Do you have a particular job title in mind?

- Describe the position you would like to have before you retire.

- Discuss your current progress toward your career goals.

- Describe where you see yourself in 10 or 20 years.

- Talk about your current career role model.

- Talk about what you hope to be doing 10 years from now – in a perfect world.

- Answer the question: "If you knew you couldn't fail, which goals would you pursue?"

Knowing your ultimate destination, and helping your mentor understand the goal you ultimately want to reach, will make it much easier for you and your mentor to work together to plot a course for success. Whether you want to change careers, lead a different company, become a motivational speaker or even retire, your mentor can help you determine what you need to do to get there.

If you aspire to be the CEO of your current employer, your path will probably be different than if you want to manage a particular business unit. However, just because you *want* to be CEO doesn't necessarily mean that your mentor will agree that you're on track to achieve your goal, or even that pursuing the role of CEO is the right track for you. Be open to the possibility that you might never have the personality, profile or pedigree to be the CEO at your current company, but know that there *is* a job for which you are perfectly suited. Perhaps being a CEO is the "right" role, but you're not at the "right" company. Perhaps you're with the "right" company, but CEO is the wrong role. Perhaps there's a different goal that better aligns with your true talents and aspirations.

Keep an open mind. Work with your mentor to understand what you want and why you want it. Get clear about your strengths and weaknesses, and listen closely to what your mentor has to say. If you both agree that your desired role is within your reach, explore the possibility that you may be able to work around your weaknesses and/or develop strategies to compensate for the experiences you lack. For example, you might gain international experience by accepting a position overseas, or add to your capabilities by learning a second or third language. Or you might seek an advanced degree at a premiere institution to enhance your resume. But also consider that the role you think you want might not be the one that will truly make you happy.

(Re)setting Expectations

What should you do if your mentor tells you that your goal is out of reach or unattainable? First, understand that they're not telling you to give up, they're likely just asking you to consider other options and alternatives for which you will be well suited. Your mentor's sole purpose is to support your goals and help you achieve them.

If you don't like what your mentor has to say, ask questions before abandoning their advice. Mentors are only privy to what we tell them, what they hear about us from others, and what they observe. So, it's possible that their observations, assumptions and conclusions may be off. Find out what they've gathered from your discussions about your background, capabilities, and your goals. You may have forgotten to mention a past position that shaped your career or created an important internal alliance that could position you well for your ultimate goal. Or perhaps your mentor isn't aware of a leadership development program that can put you on the right path, if you're accepted. Lay all the cards on the table to make sure that you have a shared appreciation for your talents, skills, experiences and preferences.

But remember, if you're paired with the right mentor, that mentor almost certainly has insights into what it will take to reach your goals. If they push back and suggest that you consider a variety of paths, you would be remiss not to listen. Open your ears and open your mind to the possibility that you may need to revisit your desires, and reevaluate your direction. Once you've had time for reflection and introspection, decide whether your long-term goals should be adjusted.

Whether the exercise results in completely new targets or simply confirms that your original goal is in fact your true aspiration, by this time, you should feel secure that you've identified your perfect path. You should also be well positioned to commit to goals for the mentorship.

How many goals should you have? Well, that depends a bit on the amount of time you plan to spend together and the nature of the goals themselves. A typical formal mentorship lasts about twelve months; it's realistic to think that you could accomplish two or three objectives during that time. For example, you might complete a communications course, work to improve your strategic thinking, and join a networking group. If these three objectives align with your long-term goals, then completing them should help you advance your career. Keep in mind that trying to tackle too many things will almost always create confusion and frustration. So, narrow your list to a manageable, achievable number. At this stage, don't worry too much about how you'll achieve each goal; that's a great topic for you and your mentor to discuss.

Your mentor should be able to help you identify the tasks and activities that align with each of your objectives. For example, let's say that your ultimate career goal is to become the Chief Financial Officer for a mid-sized firm. You have spent most of your career in purchasing, but know that to achieve your goal, you'll need balance sheet experience. So, your objective is to make a lateral move into the finance department. In working with your mentor, you might decide to take the following next steps:

- Meet with the Finance Director to assess the Department's needs (Month One)

- Interview various Finance Team members to learn more about the Department and the work they do (Month Two)

- Handle the budgeting for a high-visibility project (within the next quarter)

- Take an advanced finance course in an area that is important to, or lacking in, the company (within the first six months)

- Shadow someone in Finance who holds a position of interest (within the first eight months)

- Prepare your resume and practice interviewing skills (within the next 12 months)

If you want to become a training manager, you might:

- Share your goals with your manager during your next performance management discussion (Month One)

- Schedule a meeting with the Director of Training to discuss the needs of the Department (Month Two)

- Take a presentation skills or public speaking class (within the next three months)

- Interview others in the training department to better understand the work they do (within the next three months)

- Complete a training needs assessment for your department (within the next six months)

- Develop a training course to help individuals on your current team master a needed skill (within the next nine months)

- Participate in a training session by volunteering to assist the facilitator (within the next twelve months)

It's your mentor's responsibility to show you what you are capable of, and to help you set what they believe are realistic goals. If they push-back and suggest that you reconsider your plans, they aren't necessarily implying that you will *never* be able to realize your dream, they might simply be suggesting that you need to reevaluate your intended path. Or they might agree that your long-term goal is attainable, but may feel that plans for the next twelve months are a bit too ambitious. Regardless, be willing to make adjustments in response to your mentor's counsel. Remember that your mentor is there to direct you and support you and to guide you toward goals that matter.

Are Your Goals SMART?

Success can be summarized with a simple, straightforward formula...clarify your goals and write them down. (And of course, focus and work like heck to make them happen.) American author Brian Tracy said:

> "People with clear, written goals, accomplish far more in a shorter period of time than people without them could ever imagine."

So, when you review your goals with your mentor, recraft them to ensure that they are SMART – Specific, Measurable, Attainable, Realistic and Timely.

Specific. SMART goals are tangible and precise. Saying, "I want to increase my visibility" is not enough. It just doesn't mean much. If your goal isn't explicit, it will be difficult to put a plan in place to accomplish it, and you'll never know when you hit your mark.

Make your goals more specific by applying the Five W's. You can apply the Five W's by answering the following questions:

- <u>Wh</u>at do I want to achieve?

- <u>Wh</u>y does this goal make sense?

- <u>Wh</u>ose participation will be needed to accomplish the goal?

- <u>Wh</u>ere will I accomplish my work?

- <u>Wh</u>en will I achieve my goal?

When the Five W's are applied to the example we just discussed, it might sound something like this:

Goal: To increase my visibility this year by leading the Employee Engagement Initiative.

- "I want to become known for driving important initiatives that are meaningful to my company." (<u>Wh</u>at do I want to achieve?)

- "By taking the leadership role on a major project, I will demonstrate my capability and commitment to the organization, show that I can lead a team, and increase my visibility with senior leadership. This will help to better position me for the management role to which I aspire." (<u>Wh</u>y does this goal makes sense?)

- "My manager and my mentor." (<u>Wh</u>ose participation will be needed to accomplish the goal?)

- "I can increase my visibility by leading the Employee Engagement Initiative team." (<u>Wh</u>ere will I accomplish my work?)

- "The project starts in the second quarter and runs for 9 months." (<u>Wh</u>en will I achieve my goal?)

Measurable. A measurable goal is quantifiable, allowing progress toward the goal to be gauged based on frequency, volume, ratings, quantity, or some other criteria. "I want to sell more," is a vague goal, but there are many ways to make it more measurable. For example, you could decide to increase your sales by 15% this year, or set a goal to sell 100 additional units of a specific product. A measurable goal could include whom you hope to sell your products to. For instance, your goal could be to double your sales in the North East, or more specifically, you want to acquire two new clients in New York City. You could establish a financial objective, setting a goal to generate $500,000 in revenue within your territory this year. All of these are measurable goals, especially when associated with a particular date.

Measurable goals often include one or more of the following factors:

- Percentage improvement (15% more than the prior year)

- Numerical goal (revenue, profit, performance rank, salary increase)

- Frequency (twice a month or once a quarter)

- Quantity (increase my team by two direct reports or make four new contracts a month)

- Target date or time until success (weeks, months or years)

Attainable. For a goal to be attainable, you need to be confident that you can achieve it. Pie-in-the-sky goals are useless, if you don't think you can reach them.

Prior to 1954, experts thought it was impossible to run a 4-minute mile. People had tried for over a thousand years without success. In the 1940's, one man ran it in 4:01 minutes – a record that stood for nine years. But then, in 1954, Roger Bannister broke the 4-minute mile, running it in 3:59 minutes. He did so by setting his mind on the goal and visualizing success every day as he trained. Now, even high school runners beat the 4-minute mark.

Now, we don't run, nor do we plan to, but we do know that you can't achieve a goal if you don't believe it's possible. When something becomes possible, it becomes attainable. So, make sure that you can picture yourself reaching your goal.

Realistic. Realistic goals are those you know you can attain *and* are willing to work to achieve. Now, realistic doesn't mean that the goal is not a stretch. Stretching yourself to accomplish something that other people think isn't possible can be fun and rewarding, as long as you believe it's possible.

The key is that you have to be willing to invest the effort required to achieve your goal once it has been set. Then, make sure that you can articulate what you'll need to do to get there. Often, it's easiest to start with the end in mind and work backwards from there. What are the key milestones and what do you need to do to reach each one? Then define the steps and activities as discretely as possible.

If you break your goal down into steps and find that achieving it within your desired time frame is unrealistic, then don't give up. Take a step back and decide whether your goal is, in fact, worth pursuing. If it is, then consider how you might scale it back to make it more realistic. (This is a perfect discussion for you and your mentor.) For example, if your goal is to help a nonprofit win grant funds for an important project, it's realistic if you have a track record of winning such grants in similar amounts, and if you are willing to invest the time and effort to complete the grant application. On the other hand, if the cause is near and dear to your heart, but you've never written a grant application or have never applied for funding for such a large amount, your goal may not be realistic – at least not right now.

So, think about how you might revise the goal. Perhaps you can set an initial goal to learn how to craft a winning grant. You might work with someone experienced to get educated about the process and to get an insider's perspective on what makes a grant application appealing. With some experience under your belt, writing a grant application for your favorite nonprofit may become completely doable.

Timely. SMART goals are also timebound. In other words, they are intended to be accomplished by a certain date or within a stated time frame. Setting a date for the achievement of a goal helps to make it real and creates a sense of urgency. As businessman and author Harvey Mackay said,

"A goal is a dream with a plan and a deadline."

The real benefit of setting timely goals is that they can create positive pressure which prompts many people to take action. Dated milestones and a firm deadline give you and your mentor something to work toward and a standard against which to measure your progress. Work with your mentor to set reasonable time frames for the achievement of your goals.

Seeking Input from Others

Goal setting can be an exciting time of anticipation and hopefulness. By definition, the process requires you to think about what you want, and to narrow those "wants" down to the most important priorities. Then it requires you to get real about whether you can truly achieve your objectives in a reasonable amount of time. If you aren't sure about what you want to accomplish, or if you aren't confident that you can reach the targets you've set, you might want to invite others to weigh in.

Sometimes those around us have a better idea of what we can accomplish than we do. You might not see a goal as attainable, while your mentor can see a clear path to achievement. You might lack confidence in your abilities, while your manager sees your goal as well within your reach. On the other hand, you might have a goal in mind that's just not right for you. Sometimes, advisors, leaders, colleagues, friends and family can offer valuable insights to inform the goal setting process. So, before you finalize your goals, seek input from others.

If you work in a corporate environment, find out if you can access a survey tool or blind assessment that allows others to give honest feedback without revealing who they are. Reviewing the results can require thick skin, but perception is often reality. It can be helpful to know what people think and what they believe to be your strengths and weaknesses. Through the exercise, you might discover that your colleagues' perceptions align with your own, or you might discover some inconsistencies – flattering or unflattering. This information can help to inform your priorities.

If you don't have access to something like a 360-degree evaluation, try a do-it-yourself approach. Create a plan to seek input from a diverse group of people willing to provide candid responses. This group can include co-workers, family, and friends from many areas of your life. They can be people you know well, and people you don't.

But if you are going to make the effort to gain insights from others, be brave and include people who will speak the truth, not simply tell you what they think you want to hear. The best friends are those who will tell you that your shirt is on backwards, not those who will let you go out in public looking like a fool.

Use the insights from your focus group as data points to help you narrow your focus and refine your aspirations. Once you've refined your goals, share them with others to see how they resonate. Ultimately, if the goal excites and motivates you and you are willing to invest the effort required to achieve it, then it's likely a goal worth pursuing.

Goals May Change and That's Okay

One last thing…it's realistic to expect that some goals may change along the way. Every new experience shapes who you are and where you're headed. After working toward certain goals, you may discover that they are no longer important and may identify something else that resonates with you. That's fine. Just make sure to communicate your shift in thinking to your mentor so they can help you consider the implications of the shift, and help you plot a new course.

MENTORING IN ACTION

"In my experience, a mentor can be a guide one day, and a trusted confidant the next. Unlike your best boss, a mentor doesn't have to worry about business objectives that might influence the advice he offers. Unlike a coach, a mentor isn't focused on ensuring that you have the skills to do your job well. They don't have to monitor and inspect. To me, the mentor's most important job is to listen. The best mentors are expert listeners, but they also know what to say when you need direction," said Johnathan Reicken.

When asked to tell his story, Johnathan said, "I worked for a well-funded, start-up internet company and was on the super-fast track to the C-suite. Although I was fairly young, one of the founders took a liking to me and quickly began grooming me for success. He taught me about the business he'd been in since its infancy. He helped me learn the craft of working with, and managing others. And he helped me stay out of the politics – perhaps the most difficult challenge of them all. Although it seemed like a lofty goal, everyone knew that I would eventually move to the 'Top Floor.' It was expected, and I was working hard to be prepared.

As with most mentoring relationships, my mentor and I met on a fairly regular basis. We set some pretty definitive long-term goals and broke those down into what, at the time, seemed to be reasonable short-term goals. But then, tragedy struck my family. My daughter was diagnosed with leukemia. My world was rocked at the core, and I thought my career was in question.

Trying to hold back the tears, I shared the difficult news with my mentor, who was also the Chairman of the Board. I told him I had to take some time off and was prepared to resign, if needed. My mentor listened as I went on for more than twenty minutes without taking a breath. And then he said, "Johnathan, sometimes life throws you curves. All that's expected is that you respond and stand tall when they come." He then shared a similar story about having to take a temporary detour in his own career to care for an elderly parent.

Over the next few months, Johnathan's daughter was treated for leukemia. He took time off when he needed to, and worked part-time for a period to help his family. Johnathan's mentor checked in regularly to make sure that he was okay. When the situation stabilized, Johnathan and his mentor set aside some time to revise his career goals, extending the timelines to allow him more time for the things that were most important. Ultimately, the company was hit by the economic downturn. It was acquired by a larger firm and Johnathan left.

Today, Johnathan's daughter is free from leukemia and has a family of her own. Johnathan is the CEO of a Silicon Valley based technology company. "My mentor was there during the good times and the not-so-good times. He stood by me and gave me good counsel. It's a debt I don't think I could ever repay."

GOAL SETTING

Use this tool to refine and confirm your goals.

Part 1: Mentees with Goals

What are the goals you'd like to share with your mentor?

Goal #1:

_____

_____

_____

_____

Goal #2:

_____

_____

_____

Goal #3:

_____

_____

_____

Notes:

_____

_____

_____

_____

Part 2: Making Goals Smart-er

Work with your mentor to ensure that your goals are actionable by making them S.M.A.R.T. Select a goal from Part 1 and apply the model using the S.M.A.R.T. Chart. (See the example below.)

Goal (Example):
To improve my presentation skills within the next six months.

S.M.A.R.T. Chart			
S.M.A.R.T. Component	**Evidence**	**✓**	**Recommendation**
Specific	To improve my presentation skills		Make it more specific by stating "how" you plan to improve your skills. Add the types of skills for even greater clarity.
Measurable			Receive an "Exceptional" rating on my next Business Review presentation.
Attainable			Determine what it will take to make this goal attainable.
Realistic			Establish a plan including the steps required to achieve the goal.
Timely	within the next six months		

Further clarify the goal by adding:

- ☐ What do I want to achieve? *Achieve an "Exceptional" rating*
- ☐ Why does this goal make sense? *I will demonstrate that I am capable of being a leader*
- ☐ Whose participation will be needed to accomplish the goal? *My mentor*
- ☐ Where will I accomplish my work? *Complete the online course; practice with my mentor*
- ☐ When will I achieve my goal? *Within the next six months*

Revised goal:

To improve my presentation skills within the next six months by completing the Mastering PowerPoint course and achieving an "Exceptional" rating on my next Business Review presentation.

Use the space below to evaluate your goals.

Goal #1:

_____

_____

_____

S.M.A.R.T. Chart			
S.M.A.R.T. Component	Evidence	✓	Recommendation
Specific			
Measurable			
Attainable			
Realistic			
Timely			

Further clarify the goal by adding:

☐ What do I want to achieve?
☐ Why does this goal make sense?
☐ Whose participation will be needed to accomplish the goal?
☐ Where will I accomplish my work?
☐ When will I achieve my goal?

Revised goal:

_____

_____

_____

_____

Goal #2:

_____

_____

_____

S.M.A.R.T. Chart			
S.M.A.R.T. Component	**Evidence**	✓	**Recommendation**
Specific			
Measurable			
Attainable			
Realistic			
Timely			

Further clarify the goal by adding:

- ❑ <u>Wh</u>at do I want to achieve?
- ❑ <u>Wh</u>y does this goal make sense?
- ❑ <u>Wh</u>ose participation will be needed to accomplish the goal?
- ❑ <u>Wh</u>ere will I accomplish my work?
- ❑ <u>Wh</u>en will I achieve my goal?

Revised goal:

_____

_____

_____

_____

Goal #3:

_____

_____

_____

S.M.A.R.T. Chart			
S.M.A.R.T. Component	**Evidence**	✓	**Recommendation**
Specific			
Measurable			
Attainable			
Realistic			
Timely			

Further clarify the goal by adding:

- ☐ <u>Wh</u>at do I want to achieve?
- ☐ <u>Wh</u>y does this goal make sense?
- ☐ <u>Wh</u>ose participation will be needed to accomplish the goal?
- ☐ <u>Wh</u>ere will I accomplish my work?
- ☐ <u>Wh</u>en will I achieve my goal?

Revised goal:

_____

_____

_____

_____

Topics to discuss during the next meeting:

_____

_____

_____

_____

_____

_____

_____

_____

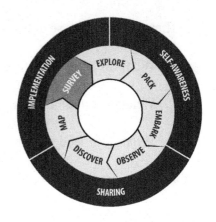

Chapter 16

SURVEY: PLAN NEXT STEPS

"Do not wait for leaders; do it alone, person to person."
—Mother Teresa

Look Back to Move Forward

Some mentoring relationships last a lifetime, but most come to a planned or natural conclusion. As you move toward the end of your mentoring journey, or simply pause for reflection, it's important to look back as you plan to move forward. As you think back on your experience, you might ask yourself the following questions:

- What did I learn from my mentor?

- What insights did I gain; what blind spots were revealed?

- Did my goals shift? If so, how?

- Have my aspirations changed? If so, in what way(s)?

- Have I been receptive to feedback from my mentor, or have I resisted? Why?

Then, consider these questions as you plan to move forward:

- What do I still need to achieve my goals?

- What do I need to change to be successful?

- What do I need to learn?

- Who can help me? How can they help?

- What do I need to do next?

In the past weeks or months, you and your mentor have reviewed your initial goals, evaluated your personal strengths and weaknesses, talked about your career history and experiences, and discussed your short- and long-term plans. During your time together, your mentor has undoubtedly offered observations and insights regarding your career path. Hopefully, you learned much about yourself through the eyes of your advisor. Now, it's up to you to make sense of their guidance and develop a plan for the future.

Keep in mind that you don't have to listen to your mentor's recommendations; after all, it's your life and your career. But remember why you entered into a mentoring relationship in the first place. Were you stuck? Were you looking for a fresh perspective? Were you hoping to benefit from the experience of someone who has been where you plan to go? As you move to the final stage of the mentoring journey, ponder the advice you received.

- Do you agree with your mentor's opinions and recommendations?

- Do you understand their perspective?

- Does their guidance make sense given your long-term objectives?

At first, the feedback might be difficult to hear. For some of us, keen observations can feel like a sharp, surprising, and unwelcome attack. But it's a mentor's job to tell you what they see with clarity and objectivity. Then, it's up to you to decide what to do with the information they shared.

Sometimes, even compliments can catch us off guard if we're not ready. Perhaps your mentor unearthed a talent you didn't know you had, or even worse, were trying to hide. Several years ago, a friend was completing his residency at a well-respected academic hospital. He worked his entire life to get to that point, and was almost ready to realize his dream of becoming a practicing physician. He sought advice from a physician friend, who ultimately became his mentor. He was undecided about whether to go into private practice, join the hospital where he had been offered a nice position, or continue with his studies and pursue a specialty much like his father had done years before. He met with his friend-turned-mentor several times a month at the hospital cafeteria. Eventually, they would meet off-site on days when he worked the early shift. The mentor listened for weeks and provided encouragement to help his friend maintain his energy as the long hours took a toll on his body and his psyche. As a diversion, the friends would talk about investing. You see, the soon-to-be-specialist was a bit of a savant in that area. One day, when our friend was particularly stressed, the mentor asked his friend a poignant and challenging question, "Is this really what you want to do?" The question stopped the young man in his tracks.

Mentee: "Why would you ask that? Becoming a physician is all I've ever wanted."

Mentor: "Okay, that may be true. But I've been a physician for 20 years. I know what it takes to do this job. I know the upsides and the downsides. I know how the profession has changed, and I know that it will continue to change. As I look at you, I see an incredibly capable individual who would make a fine physician. But, at the same time, I wonder if the career is right for you."

Mentee: "What? You don't think I can handle it? I work at the hospital all day, and sometimes all night. Then, I go back home and study, only to wake up and do it all over again. I was first in my class, and I'm not sure there's anyone else in this residency program who is more committed than I am."

Mentor: "Do I think you can handle it? Absolutely. You've proven that. But do I think your career choice will bring you joy? Will you look back 20 years from now and be happy with your decision to go into private practice, or to take the position at the hospital, or to continue your medical education? I wonder.

"How many times have we met for a cup of coffee?"

Mentee: "Ten, maybe fifteen."

Mentor: "How many times has that cup of coffee turned into an hour-long therapy session?"

Mentee: "A few more times than I'd like to admit."

Mentor: "Here's how I see it. You're good at your job...maybe even great at it. You are kind and conscientious. You are competent and skilled. You have all of the characteristics of a good physician, and Lord knows we need more of those. However, when we talk about medicine, you look down. You put your hand on your forehead, squint your eyes, and wring your hands. You're almost always exhausted. In fact, you are on your way to the hospital now, and I know it's risky, but I must say, you look like you haven't had a moment's sleep.

"But what really stands out is how frustrated you become when you talk about hospital politics and dealing with the bureaucracy. I am here to tell you that it's not going to get any better.

"Can I ask you a question?"

Mentee: "Sure."

Mentor: "A few months ago, we talked about your reasons for getting into medicine. You said you wanted to follow in your dad's footsteps. I get that. I became a doctor for the very same reason, and I'm glad that I did. But it's not an easy path, especially if you don't love it at the core of your being. It requires long hours, time away from your family, and you'll find yourself in a boatload of debt that can bury you for years."

Mentee: "Well, aren't you the voice of gloom and doom."

Mentor: "Look, I'm just telling you the truth…and this is coming from a guy who loves his job. For me, there was no alternative. It's what I was meant to do. But when I listen to you talk about investments, your eyes light up. You lean forward. You exude a completely different energy that, frankly, makes me want to give it all up and go to Wall Street.

"As long as you're in medicine, I'll always be here to mentor you and offer advice. I'll continue to share my experience and my thoughts. In fact, I'll tell you right now that if you continue down this path I think you should pursue a specialty. But if you aren't sure – I mean really sure – that you want to be a physician or a surgeon, I'd suggest that you think long and hard about your next steps."

The mentor's candor caught our friend off guard. Frankly, it stopped him in his tracks. He had already invested so much in becoming a physician, and he was right there. He was about to turn his ambition into reality. But it wasn't what *he* really wanted. A few months after this pivotal conversation, our friend completed his residency and then headed to business school. He's now a successful financial investor living in New York City, and living his true dream.

So, what's the message in all of this? Keep an open mind, and then listen to your heart. A mentor can tell you what they see, but ultimately the decisions are up to you. You determine what's worth working for. You set your goals, and you're the one who has to wake up every day and work toward them.

Getting On the Same Page

Sometimes mentors offer specific examples and provide clear direction to inform your next steps. They can help you craft plans that describe your every move in detail. But often, their advice is a bit less direct. For example, your mentor might make an observation followed with an insight about how a behavior they've observed may be impacting others' perceptions of you. Is your mentor telling you that you have developed a bad reputation, or are they simply making you aware of the impact your actions might be having on others? It's important to clarify.

It is possible to think you understand what your mentor is telling you, yet totally miss the point. Whether your mentor offers obvious statements or subtle hints, to make the most progress in your mentorship, you need to train yourself to hear both. Last week, when your mentor asked if you copied your boss on the progress report you sent to your team, did you simply say, "No, she didn't ask to see it"? Or did you think about why your mentor might have posed the question in the first place? Perhaps your mentor was suggesting that there's value in copying your boss on all of your reports so that she can see the quality of work you're producing. It's easy to jump to conclusions about the meaning behind a comment or question, but you won't really understand your mentor's intent unless you make a habit of asking clarifying questions. If you want to know more about a comment made by your mentor, you might clarify by asking questions like:

- What did you mean when you said...?

- Do you think I should have...? Why?

- Can you tell me more about...?

- How might that have helped me?

- What could I do differently?

- Do you think that was a good/bad idea?

In addition to making sure you are truly hearing what your mentor has to say, you must also be sure that they are hearing you. If your mentor is to discover what's holding you back, they must understand where you've been. In addition to sharing facts about your background, as you did early in the relationship, it's also important to talk about how you think, how you approach decisions, and what affects the way in which you take action toward meeting your goals. Sharing your thought process will help your mentor understand the assumptions you're making and discover the misconceptions that are holding you back.

Sometimes offering examples is the best way to be sure you're giving your mentor all the information they need. For instance, when discussing how you arrived at your current plan, you might explain the process you used to determine your next steps and the thinking behind your priorities. If you share more than they need to know, they'll tell you, but don't be offended. It's better to share more than is necessary, and be cut off, than to hold back and miss out on key points. To confirm that your mentor has heard you, check for understanding by asking questions like:

- What did you hear in what I just said?

- What are your observations about the process I went through to...?

- Would you have approached the decision/problem/opportunity differently? If so, how?

- What advice do you have?

What Have You Learned?

Every mentee moves through the mentoring cycle at a different pace. You may have arrived at this stage after a few weeks or a few months, or it may have taken a year or even several years to get to where you are today. The speed with which one progresses through a mentorship can be influenced by many factors, including: the complexity of one's goals, the level of trust between the mentor and the mentee, and the time each party has to invest in the pursuit. Regardless of how long it has taken you to get to this point, it's now time to take stock in the relationship and ruminate on what you've learned so far.

First, document your progress and list your accomplishments. Did you tackle the goals you had hoped to? Did you learn something new? Can you check some things off your list? Remember, mentoring is often more about incremental improvements than it is about monumental leaps – although transformational realizations and quantum leaps are possible. So, look through your journal and highlight your successes, both large and small.

Then, assess your relationship. In a perfect world, every mentorship would result in a lifetime of insights, honesty and support, but that's not always the case. Sometimes, we only need a mentor for a short period of time. Sometimes, we simply just don't click, and sometimes the timing just doesn't work out. More often than not, though, a mentoring relationship can offer a unique opportunity to learn something about yourself from someone who has experiences to share. As you move into the Survey stage, think about your relationship with your current mentor. Evaluate what's working, and be honest about what's not. If you're at the end of your journey, make a decision to learn from the experience, the good and the bad. Your learnings could translate to selection criteria for a future mentoring relationship.

The Pace of Progress

In addition to reviewing how much you've accomplished since you began working with your mentor, take a look back at the pace at which you've progressed. Did you achieve your goal within the agreed upon time frame? Or did you reach your objectives more slowly/quickly than expected? If you didn't reach your goal on schedule, to what do you attribute the delay? If you met your goal sooner than you anticipated, what enabled you to progress so quickly? Has the delay/acceleration impacted your ability to achieve your long-term objectives?

Slower-than-anticipated progress could signal a bigger issue. You might be stuck and haven't been able to figure out a solution to your current situation, or you might just need a little help breaking a larger goal into manageable tasks. Take the time to think through everything that needs to occur in order to reach your next milestone. Identify your target accomplishment and set a date by which you will achieve it. Your mentor can offer guidance in working through the steps that can lead you to success and may suggest avenues that you haven't considered.

But slower-than-expected progress could also indicate a lack of motivation to achieve your stated goals or a conflict between the life you say you want and the priorities that drive your daily actions. Now, don't rush to conclude that we're saying you're lazy! Just like our friend, the aspiring physician, you might be working toward a goal that you don't *really* want. When your heart and mind are in conflict, it can be difficult to move forward. Likewise, it can be difficult to move forward if your priorities are in conflict with your aspirations.

We both have families. We are moms and entrepreneurs. We want to grow our business and we secretly (or not so secretly) want to make a difference in the world. But sometimes, our goals hit our reality head on. When sitting in the carline at school waiting to retrieve your seven-year-old, for example, it can be difficult to imagine yourself standing in a board room facilitating a discussion about a change initiative that will impact the destiny of a Fortune 100 company. Sometimes you've gotta do what you've gotta do, but you can't let your daily responsibilities interfere with your life's purpose. Instead, set goals in all of the important areas of your life, or you'll never achieve balance and satisfaction.

In the early chapters of this book, we talk about the differences between a coach and a mentor. A coach helps you learn new skills, while a mentor helps you achieve more holistic goals. Your mentor can help you navigate potential conflicts between your priorities, while aligning your efforts in *all* of the important areas of your life. You won't get an award for impressing your mentor, so don't try to. Instead, provide context. Talk about your work life, yes. Talk about your career, yes. But also share information about your family, your hobbies, and other important goals. Ultimately, you'll reflect on those moments in the carline with joyful contemplation, just as you'll celebrate your major career achievements.

Mentor Your Mentor

You may not realize it, but your mentor will likely value your feedback and guidance as a mentee, just as you value their insight and advice. Most mentors volunteer to guide others because they truly want to help make a difference in someone else's career. But while their motives are good, not all mentors are trained to effectively offer advice.

For example, you may have found that your mentor is not exactly adept at delivering bad news. When they told you that you were, once again, not accepted into the management development program, they did so with the same level of empathy as the representative investigating overcharges on your cell phone bill. For your mentor, getting into the management development program may be only one way to increase your visibility on the path to your career goal and, therefore, your rejection letter might not seem significant. But for you, a second denial might be the final blow that prompts you to consider giving up on your goals altogether.

Rest assured that most mentors want to motivate you toward achievement, not take the wind out of your sails. So, it's important to help them understand how to tailor their messages for the greatest outcome. When discussing your mentoring experience, you might:

- Share your reactions to their counsel

- Offer ideas that could aid your mentor in working with other mentees

- Acknowledge and appreciate their observations and insights, and offer feedback on how the information was delivered

- Tell them what they do well

- Suggest an alternative approach, when appropriate

You need a mentor who is willing to be informative, communicative, and encouraging, as well as brutally honest when unabashed honesty is called for. Your career is not helped when your mentor fails to share key facts about your reputation or let you in on the real reason why you didn't get the promotion you were aiming for. You need to know what they know. So, if your mentor seems unable to speak their mind without filtering what they say, it's in your interest to encourage them to speak the truth, even if it hurts a bit.

In addition to their delivery, there may be other things your mentor could work on, such as: their availability, the specificity of feedback they offer you, their willingness to plug you into their network when it makes sense, or their comfort level in serving as a champion for your career, among other things. But unless you share your needs with your mentor and offer them the same candid feedback that you expect, they will never be able to improve their own skills and will never become a better mentor for you and for future mentees.

Often, mentees wait until they've achieved their goals or have come to the end of a pre-established mentoring program before they offer feedback to their mentor. But don't wait. If you feel that you and your mentor would both benefit from your insights, then offer them immediately. Most mentors are thick-skinned and more than willing to listen, but like all of us, they might have a blind spot or two.

Of course, you'll want to be sure to offer feedback kindly and respectfully. If you are uncomfortable having potentially difficult situations, you might start by reviewing all the ways your mentor has helped your career, and then lead into some ways you think your mentor might have approached situations differently. In other words, start with the positive, bring up the negative, and then end on a positive note. If you sense that you've offended your mentor in any way, apologize, clarify, and emphasize that your observations and expectations may be unique to you.

Regardless of where you are in an established mentorship, take time to thank your mentor for investing in you. Often, formal mentorships evolve into informal relationships and friendships that can last for decades. If it's time to conclude your formal mentoring relationship, then end on a high note, in the spirit of true and genuine gratitude.

MENTORSHIP SURVEY

Use this tool to reflect on the time you've spent with your mentor to date and to plan next steps.

Number of meetings so far: _____
Time remaining in the mentorship: _____

Part 1: Strength of the Mentoring Relationship
Themes/trends observed over time:

_____

_____

_____

_____

_____

Use the space below to evaluate the mentoring relationship at the current time based on the Success Factors.

Statement	Assessment				
	Never	Rarely	Occasionally	Frequently	Always
My mentor listens to what I have to say.					
My mentor truly understands me and my long-term goals.					
My mentor has been helpful in tackling a short-term goal.					
My mentor believes that I can be successful in achieving my goals.					

Statement	Assessment				
	Never	Rarely	Occasionally	Frequently	Always
My mentor provides candid and honest feedback.					
My mentor is respectful even during difficult conversations.					
I feel comfortable sharing confidential information.					
I can be honest and open with my mentor.					
My mentor is receptive to feedback and acts on it to improve the relationship.					
I have grown through mentoring.					
Overall, I am satisfied with the mentoring relationship.					

Feedback for my mentor:

- One thing my mentor does particularly well:
- One thing my mentor could do differently:

Additional feedback for my mentor:

_____

_____

_____

_____

_____

_____

Part 2: Next Steps
Our mentorship:

❏ Is coming to a
close and will end
on __/__/__

❏ Will continue
through __/__/__

❏ Has an unclear future

_____

_____

_____

_____

Topics to discuss during the next meeting:

_____

_____

_____

_____

_____

_____

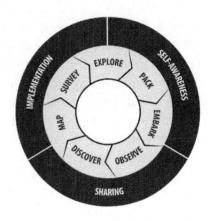

Chapter 17

WHAT'S NEXT?

"Be willing to be a beginner every single morning."
—*Meister Eckhart*

The End of the Journey

Congratulations! You made your way through the mentoring journey. You moved from Self-Awareness to Implementation and through Follow-Up. You likely learned a lot about yourself along the way, and that alone warrants a pat on the back.

As you maneuvered through the cycle, you may have received just the push you needed to accelerate your development. Perhaps you identified a weakness that you were able to successfully overcome, or maybe you uncovered a latent fear that needed to be addressed. You might have hit a plateau or two that caused you to stall for a bit, but persevered and ended with a breakthrough. You might have adjusted your plans to adapt to guidance provided by your mentor, or you may have discovered a newfound commitment to your initial aspiration. Regardless of the nature of your journey, you are no doubt better positioned for victory than you were prior to meeting your mentor.

Mentoring relationships generally follow a circular pattern, beginning with discussions about dreams and aspirations, progressing over time as goals are realized, and culminating with new intentions and targets. Some mentor/mentee relationships may continue for a life-time, while others may be short-lived, formed only to help you move forward in your quest. But most mentorships – long or short – help us learn something important about ourselves.

With any luck, you and your mentor have moved from friendly ac-quaintances to trusted comrades. You've probably gotten used to your mentor's style and approach. You can likely anticipate their reactions long before they have them. And your mentor has probably come to know your own preferences, tendencies and quirks. Odds are you have very different personalities, communication styles, and views on life, but even with all that, you have probably come to know and respect each other.

Together, you established a rhythm (meeting weekly, bimonthly or monthly), and a preferred method of communication – in person, phone, via skype or via email. You might have discovered that you prefer to meet off-site where you can't be bothered by interruptions or tempted by other responsibilities. You might have found that your mentor appreciates a text letting him know how things are going, as opposed to a lengthy email with "too much" detail. You might have agreed that sugarcoating feedback is a waste of time for both of you, and that you both relish the freedom of being able to offer unfiltered feedback when appropriate. By now, your partnership has undoubt-edly become characterized by its own unique DNA. It's unlikely that you will ever experience a future mentorship in exactly the same way.

Our hope is that you are exiting this moment in time with fond memories and important lessons…even if the lessons were tough to learn. That said, now is not the time to stop growing! On the contrary. As you approach the chasm between Survey and Explore, it's time to determine what it will take to make a quantum leap toward your destiny, and it's time to commit to a new set of challenging goals. Now is the time to reflect on your progress and to begin to look ahead to the future.

Beginning, Again

Speak with your mentor about the transition, and develop a plan to ensure that you are well-positioned to take your next steps. Those next steps will be critical, especially if you have come to depend on your mentor for advice, support and motivation. As you're setting new goals and perhaps embarking on a new path, talk about the skills that you will need to further advance your career, discuss the information that will help you move forward, and identify the resources you'll need to support your efforts. If you have made a strong connection with your mentor and feel that you will benefit from continued communication and support, ask if they would be open to extending the mentorship. If they agree, then use your time to envision the next phase of mentoring. Challenge your mentor and challenge yourself to push farther, move faster, or go bigger. If, on the other hand, you both feel that it's best to move on, seek your mentor's insights and try to envision your next best mentor.

But if you've met your goals, and you are truly ready to move to the next step, examine your needs to determine whether you need a mentor or would benefit even more from a sponsor. A sponsor is an individual with visibility and position, who can influence others and advocate on your behalf. Sponsors are willing to risk their own reputations and careers for your success. Visit our website (www.metajourn. com) for more information on sponsorship and how it can help in your career journey. (Note: It's not unusual to be in need of a mentor and a sponsor at some point in your career.)

Closing the Books

As you near the end of the mentorship, reflect on how far you've come. Did you break through a barrier that used to stand in your way? Did you overcome a fear to accomplish a goal? Are you better at standing strong in the face of a challenge? Did you move beyond your insecurities, come out of your shell, or step out of obscurity to make a name for yourself? Did you learn to embrace your strengths and minimize your weaknesses? Did you shift your focus from dreaming to making your dreams come true?

If you moved even the slightest bit or grew by even the tiniest amount, then you benefitted from mentoring. Maybe you learned that you are destined for leadership, or realized what you really want is to excel as an individual contributor. Keep in mind that you might not truly appreciate all the benefits of your mentoring experience until years from now when you have the opportunity to reflect on the road you traveled, the doors you opened, and the route you took on the way to the pinnacle of your career.

A mentor can help you move forward in the face of a setback. A mentor can give you the confidence you need to reach your true potential. A mentor will be honest when others are telling you what you want to hear. A mentor can help you find the right path when you feel lost or off course. A mentor will inspire you to act when you'd rather sit and ponder. A mentor will offer the kind of advice and direction that only a been-there-done-that kind of person can. A mentor will ask questions that will challenge your thinking and force you to face the truths that might ultimately alter your plans. A mentor will show you the way with their actions and will guide you through the lens of their own experience; their path might serve as a blueprint for your own life and career. A mentor will help you identify and recruit others to support your efforts and help you achieve your goals. The benefits of mentoring are endless.

Being a mentor is perhaps one of the best gifts that an individual can give to another, and being a mentee is the chance to learn and grow beyond what you ever thought possible.

"Every new beginning comes from some
other beginning's end." —Seneca

MENTORING IN ACTION

We have spent over 25 years in the business arena, and have faced many challenges. At one time, we believed that the key to success was hard work. But throughout our careers we've learned that hard work, alone, is never enough. Committed work, in the wrong direction, will not get you to your destination.

The mentors who have helped us along the way, were – and are – brave enough to offer honest and direct feedback. They have helped us to unlock our true potential, and to create plans to realize our dreams. They have picked us up when we have fallen, and have cheered for our accomplishments. Yet, they have been tough when they needed to be. They have told us things that were hard to hear, and have talked us through difficult decisions that have tested our courage and determination.

Because of them, we have accomplished things we had hoped for, but secretly never thought were possible. We have learned lessons that we never could have learned in business school, and we have had opportunities beyond our wildest dreams. We have also avoided some pretty major hazards that could have put us in peril, and have grown from mistakes we've made along the way.

Could we have achieved the same success on our own? Absolutely not. We owe a true debt of gratitude to the mentors who have helped us throughout our lives. There is no relationship like a mentoring relationship. There is no greater gift than the gift of unconditional support.

TRANSITION PLAN

Use this tool to reflect on your experience as a mentee, and prepare for the next phase of your journey.

Part 1: Looking Back

What have you learned from this mentoring experience?

_____

_____

_____

_____

_____

_____

_____

What would you change if you could do it all over again?

_____

_____

_____

_____

_____

_____

_____

Part 2: Moving Forward

What are your goals moving forward? (What do you want to learn, do or be?)

_____

_____

_____

_____

_____

_____

Who can help you achieve your goals?

_____

_____

_____

_____

_____

What are your next steps?

_____

_____

_____

_____

_____

_____

_____

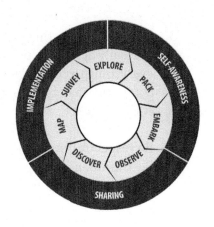

Chapter 18

MAKING THE MOST OF YOUR RELATIONSHIP

"If you cannot see where you are going, ask someone who has been there before."
—J. Loren Norris

Best Practices

A successful mentoring relationship can alter your career path and positively impact your life. Therefore, it's important to take your relationship as seriously as your day job. As you prepare to embark on your own mentoring journey, keep these best practices in mind.

1. Let your mentor take charge during the early stages of the mentoring process, but be prepared to take the reins as the mentorship develops. A mentor can drive the agenda and conversations initially, but they will eventually look to you to own the relationship.

2. Prepare and share your career goals, objectives and plans with your mentor. Then, ask for their observations, insights, and guidance. Remain flexible and open to their recommendations.

3. Commit to meeting with your mentor on a regular basis at a mutually agreed-upon time. Don't expect your mentor to drop everything to counsel you every time a situation or opportunity comes up; instead, proactively schedule your meetings at their convenience.

4. Be respectful. Arrive on time and prepared for every meeting. Be thorough with your communications, without being too long-winded, and make the best use of your time together.

5. Use a journal to take notes during your meetings. Capture your thoughts, questions, action items and next steps. Review your notes regularly to stay on track.

6. Openly share both your successes and your failures. If you only discuss what you did right, you'll never get feedback and advice on how to avoid missteps.

7. Ask for and remain open to feedback. Listen without becoming defensive or upset. Keep in mind that your mentor is being honest in an effort to be helpful. Glossing over your weaknesses won't help you in the long run.

8. Be specific when making requests or asking for help. Most mentors aren't clairvoyant. So, be clear and direct, but remember, your mentor has the right to say "no" when asked.

9. Avoid whining and complaining to your mentor. Not only does bellyaching damage your professional reputation, it can be difficult for a mentor to provide objective advice when you're being very subjective.

10. Honor your commitments. Follow up and follow through by taking action toward your goals between meetings with your mentor. Always let your mentor know when you follow their advice.

11. Mentor your mentor. Let them know how they can best work with you to achieve optimal results. Don't let your mentor's style

prevent you from hearing what they have to say, and never say anything to others that could damage your mentor's reputation.

12. Keep your conversations private. Always maintain confidences to foster trust and expect your mentor to do the same.

13. Seek to learn from every mentoring relationship and always end a time-bound mentorship on a positive note. Mentoring relationships may extend for many years. Some endure for a lifetime, so keep the door open.

14. Show your appreciation. Find ways to thank them and let them know how much you value their time and attention.

15. When the opportunity presents itself, return the favor by mentoring someone else.

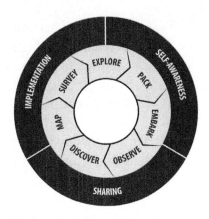

Epilogue

WHAT'S NEXT?

In this book we've described the process that shapes successful mentoring relationships from the perspectives of both the mentor and mentee. Now, it's your turn to truly discover the power of mentoring.

You have the opportunity to make an immense difference in your life and in the lives of others. Even if your workplace does not have a formal mentoring program in place, you can be the spark that starts a mentoring movement! Armed with the information contained in this book, and a passion for mentoring, you can take the first step. If your organization already has a mentoring program in place, you can help to make it stronger by using and sharing some of the tools and techniques we've covered.

We are often asked about the components of an effective mentoring program. Through our work, we've found that the most successful mentoring programs contain the following components:

- A dedicated program manager

- Diagnostic tools to assess needs

- Formal pairing of program participants based on established criteria

- Structured frameworks and processes for all program components (ex. Mentor/mentee selection, mentor/mentee matching, goal setting, ongoing evaluation, transitioning, etc.)

- Classroom and/or web-based training for mentors and mentees

- An integrated system for assessing program effectiveness and demonstrating a return on investment, where applicable

- Trainer and Master Mentor certification to support and sustain the mentoring program

Workplace Benefits

We have been fortunate to help many organizations, educational institutions, and associations build strong, sustainable mentoring programs. And we have had the pleasure of witnessing, firsthand, the benefits of mentoring in the workplace. Some of these benefits include:

- Higher levels of employee engagement

- Increased employee satisfaction

- Greater retention of high potential employees

- Advocacy and enhanced visibility for diverse populations

- Opportunities for cross-organization visibility

- Leader accountability for talent development

- Ability to attract top talent

- Improved communication across geographic and cultural boundaries

- Natural translation of the company culture and values

Attracting and retaining top talent will continue to be one of the greatest challenges for leaders across the globe. The talent strategies of the world's largest and most effective organizations will almost certainly include mentoring. Organizations of all sizes and structures will take note. Mentoring and sponsorship programs are already becoming part of the employer value proposition for job seekers. Employees appreciate and will come to expect the investment in their development.

Mentoring Trends

So what does the future hold for mentoring? One thing we know for sure is that mentoring will continue to adapt in response to the evolving landscape. A peek into our crystal ball (and a review of a ton of trending data) reveals the following trends:

A New Definition

Not too long ago, many definitions for the term "mentoring" referenced a relationship between an older mentor and a younger mentee. But times have changed, and definitions have evolved to define a mentoring relationship as one between an experienced mentor and a less experienced mentee. In part, this shift was due to the growing use of technology in the workplace, and the need to find ways to help employees keep up with the latest technological advancements.

While veteran mentors mentoring younger staff members has been commonplace for decades, the emergence of younger mentors is a newer phenomenon, and a trend that will almost certainly continue. As employees age, mentoring will help bridge the gap between the generations. Senior level leaders who have grown up in the industry will use mentoring as a way to transfer valuable knowledge and experience before retiring. But mentoring will also provide a forum for those who are technically savvy (and likely younger) to impart their wisdom to those who may not have grown up as digital natives.

Mentoring Millennials

Although there is some disagreement among experts when differentiating between the generations, Millennials are generally defined as those born between 1977 and 1997 (*Harvard Business Review, May,*

2010). It is projected that eighty-six million Millennials will be in the workplace by 2020, representing 40% of the total working population *(Forbes, January, 2014).*

Research shows that Millennials derive greater levels of satisfaction from mentoring than from other workplace benefits, including increases in salary and incentive compensation. *(Harvard Business Review, May, 2010)*According to the Harvard Business Review, Millenials want their boss to:

- Help them navigate their career path

- Give them straight feedback

- Coach and mentor them

- Sponsor them for formal development programs

- Offer flexible schedules

And they want their company to:

- Help them develop skills for the future

- Have strong values

- Offer customizable options in their benefit/rewards package

- Allow them to blend work with the rest of their life

- Offer a clear career path

Of course, not all organizations will be able to afford their Millennials everything on the lists, but they can align them with qualified mentors who can help them create a path to success by acclimating them to the company and culture, and helping to groom them for future roles. Companies looking to attract and retain the most talented Millennials are taking note by offering comprehensive professional development programs and opportunities for advancement. Formalized mentoring programs will become a necessity for those companies seeking a competitive edge.

One Size Does Not Fit All

Although it's important to have a consistent mentoring framework, differences in culture, vision, mission, and strategic priorities warrant customization of program components. It's important to understand that a "one size fits all" approach does not work for today's complex organizations. Building a custom mentoring program involves understanding your organization's unique needs and customizing the mentoring solution to align to your strategic imperatives. For example, companies that offer the option to work remotely may require opportunities for self-study and may need systems to virtually connect mentors with their mentees.

More Will Mentor

At one time most mentoring relationships were developed organically through interpersonal connections. As mentor matching became more formalized, it was often reserved for high-potentials or offered as an extra benefit for those who already had an accelerated ticket to the C-Suite. However, in recent years we have seen mentoring shift from a limited, controlled audience to a broad benefit for the massive middle. This trend will continue as more and more employees seek professional development and career pathing.

A Critical Talent Strategy

Organizations of all shapes and sizes will continue to expand on their talent management systems to address employees' needs across the development continuum. These comprehensive, integrated efforts will help build skills that benefit employees at all levels, while supporting a culture of promotion, diversity, and inclusion.

Companies are beginning to differentiate between the many roles that can help their employees acquire the knowledge and skills they need to succeed. Roles that were once intermingled – the role of Coach, Mentor and Sponsor – are now more clearly defined, enabling organizations to appropriately align and leverage their resources to accelerate employee development.

When an employee begins a new job, the focus is likely to be on mastering the skills needed to be successful in the position. A <u>coach</u> can provide the information and direct feedback needed to promote the necessary skill development. However, when the individual has become comfortable in their position, they can shift their focus to longer-term goals. At this point, the individual will likely benefit from a <u>mentor</u> who can offer career guidance and support. As the employee moves closer to key positions, <u>sponsors</u> can offer increased visibility and advocacy to advance their career.

Mentoring is an important accelerator for developing high-potentials and readying them for sponsorship. The role of the mentor changes as top talent moves closer to their ultimate career goals. The nearer the individual is to promotion, the greater the need for sponsorship.

Based on current trends, we predict that talent-focused organizations will continue to look for ways to leverage training and education, as well as valuable people resources, in an effort to entice and motivate top talent.

Be the Spark!

Wherever you are in your journey – whether you have just landed your first real job, or are an entrepreneur looking to grow your business, or are hoping to hold a leadership position in a prominent trade association – you'll always have something to learn from an experienced mentor. If you are affiliated with an organization that offers a formal mentoring program, take advantage of the gift. Make it known that you want to be a mentee, and then make the most of the opportunity.

Likewise, if you have something to give to others, we challenge you to become a mentor and share your experience with someone else. You can help a mentee by guiding them to an appropriate career path that aligns with their goals, and can share lessons learned to help them avoid potential pitfalls. Again, if your organization has an established mentoring program, take advantage of it and offer your time to a mentee.

If, however, your organization does not offer mentoring, then venture out on your own. If you are looking for a mentor, identify the characteristics you are looking for, let others know that you want to be mentored, and proactively approach potential candidates. If you want to be a mentor, assess your own strengths and determine what you can offer a mentee. Then, keep an eye out for individuals who might benefit from your experience and expertise. Who knows, you might just spark a mentoring revolution!

We wish you nothing but incredible success on your professional journey.

RESOURCES

Below is an example of a Mentoring Agreement that can be used to help set realistic expectations during the initial mentoring meeting.

Mentoring Agreement

By signing this agreement, we are voluntarily entering into a mentoring relationship that we expect to be mutually beneficial. We want this to be a rich experience with the majority of our time spent on substantive development activities.

We agree:
- To be dedicated to the program for the full _____ months.
- To meet face-to-face _____ times per month for the first _____ months of the program.
- To communicate weekly via email or phone.
- To maintain confidentiality.
- _____
- _____
- _____
- _____

Additional comments:

_____

_____

_____

_____

_____

_____
Mentor Signature / Date

_____
Print Name

_____
Mentee Signature / Date

_____
Print Name

Through our years of research and working with clients, we have found that successful mentoring programs contain the following components:

Component
Gap Analysis: Program design is based on a thorough analysis of business needs, matching the organization's business strategy to its talent strategy.
Executive Support: Program champion is selected and expectations are clearly outlined.
Journey Development: Program design includes clearly defined goals, expectations, disciplined processes and a detailed project plan.
Project Team: Program Champion, leadership and core team engage in development to understand program components and offer insights.
Recruitment Strategy: Program lead identifies target groups for program levels (emerging leaders, executive leadership, diversity and inclusion)
Marketing Strategy: Program lead develops the program marketing plan including branding, promotion and specific touch points.
Communication Plan: Program lead provides ongoing communications to further embed and sustain program.
Matching Process: Program lead along with core team members ensure that matching is based on relevant criteria.
Training Plan: Program lead provides foundational, advanced and ongoing training for Mentor/ Mentees.
Program Launch: Program lead launches program with established standards, processes and expectations.

Matching Process:
Program lead along with core team members ensure that matching is based on relevant criteria.

Ongoing Support:
Program lead provides ongoing resources to support overall program goals in order to create a sustainable program.

Measure Effectiveness:
Program lead collects and analyzes data. Recommendations utilize a variety of sources for program improvements and Mentor/ Mentee practices.

Executive Summary:
Program lead provides a summary of program analysis, outcomes, key learnings, return on investment and plans for sustaining the program.

Transition:
Program lead collaborates with the core team and reviews data for program improvements. Master Mentors are trained to facilitate future skill building sessions.

The following survey should be used to identify your current needs (coach, mentor, sponsor).

Count the number of checks for the *within a year* and *right now* category in each of the shaded (dark grey, light grey, and cream) areas.

Career Checkup

NEEDS	Not At All	In Two to Three Years	Within A Year	Right Now
Increased Visibility				
High-Level Networks				
Accelerated Development				
Credible Testimonials				
Image Development				
Career Guidance				
Ethical and Moral Guidance				
Professional Identity				
Role Model for Values and Behaviors				
Navigating Office Politics				
Direct Feedback				
Skill Development				
Problem Solving				
Confidence				
Help Filling a Knowledge Gap				

The area that you scored the highest in is indicative of the role that you currently need the most.

Dark Grey= Sponsor

Light Grey= Mentor

Cream= Coach

About Metajourn

Metajourn is a management consulting firm helping businesses, educational institutions, governmental entities and Nonprofits reach their full potential.

Our clients' needs are as diverse and unique as they are. There is no "one size fits all" approach, and there certainly isn't a universal set of prebuilt solutions to address each of their needs. Over the years, though, we've developed a portfolio of processes, tools and methodologies that enable us to quickly diagnose their issues, and engage their teams in implementable solutions that achieve results.

We work with clients around the world in a broad range of industries. We believe that to be successful in today's complex environment, organizations must be grounded in a clear purpose, guided by a well-articulated mission, and shepherded by strong leadership. Revenues, profitability and value are the natural outcome of a customer-centric business. Knowledge of the customer, customer engagement, organizational alignment, and a united workforce are at the root of a meaningful customer experience.

To learn more about how we can help you achieve sustainable results, please visit our website www.metajourn.com or email us at:

Hayley, Hnorman@metajourn.com
Stephanie, Smelnick@metajourn.com

We look forward to hearing from you soon!

Your Transformation Partners
Building lasting capability that leads to rapid
performance improvement and sustainable results.

CPSIA information can be obtained
at www.ICGtesting.com
Printed in the USA
BVOW09*0224210917
494862BV00001B/1/P